A unique teacher of the pros shows you how to

PLAY LOWER HANDICAP GOLF

by Phil Rodgers with Al Barkow

Photographs by Steve Szurlej

A **GOLF DIGEST** BOOK

Published by Golf Digest/Tennis, Inc.
A New York Times Company
5520 Park Avenue
Post Office Box 0395
Trumbull, Connecticut 06611-0395

Trade book distribution by
Simon & Schuster, A Division
Simon & Schuster, Inc.
Simon & Schuster Building
Rockefeller Center
1230 Avenue of the Americas
New York, New York 10020

First printing, 1986
ISBN: 0-914178-63-6
Library of Congress: 84-63138
Printed in the United States of America

Cover and book design by Karen Fecenko-Lyon
Printing and binding by R. R. Donnelley

This book is dedicated to my mother, Winnifred, and to Beverley Marie, Vivian Louise and to my lovely wife Karen Lee.

FOREWORD

I'll always have a soft spot for Phil Rodgers for reasons that go far beyond all the help he's given me with my golf game in recent years. Although we are mighty different in a lot of ways, in others we are cut from very similar cloth.

As a kid playing junior and then amateur golf at the national level, I had a bent for directness and brashness that sometimes got me in hot water, but no matter how bad I was I could always point to someone worse. Phil in those days was just about the cockiest, most irreverent, feistiest little son of a gun who ever swung a club. He was good, and he knew it, and he let you know he knew it. Everyone wanted to beat his brains out, and no one more than me. The additional problem was that we were both blond and crew-cut and on the hefty side, so sometimes people would confuse us and get made at me thinking I was that other guy. Boy, could he get people's dander up! And, of course, he can still hit the spot with the needle when he has a mind to, which is one reason I still so much enjoy his company.

Our early battles continued well beyond the golf course, too. No one I've met has enjoyed eating more than me, but Philamon Rodgers had my measure. Hard and long as I shovelled, Phil always got me in the end. I'll never forget the evening, staying as young amateurs in the Crow's Nest above the Augusta National clubhouse for the Masters, when we ate the place clean out of chateaubriands. We were both rationed after that, but I swear it was Phil who did most of the damage.

Much companionship and fun as Phil and I have enjoyed both on the course and off, the bond that has as really deepened our friendship as time has passed is our mutual fascination with golf technique. Phil is one of those people who will still be working on a better way to swing the golf club if he lives to be a hundred, and I'm the same. We may never solve all the mysteries this game presents, but neither of us will ever stop trying.

I got my first insights into Phil's precocious knowledge of technique during his Tour days, when it was winning him tournaments, sometimes at my expense. But for the real McCoy I had to wait until 1980, the year I decided either to revitalize my game or quit, and asked Phil for help. I discovered that good player as he was, he had become an even better teacher, and especially of the short game.

My successes later that year, and the better times I've had since, owe a great deal to our sessions. In fact, if I can finally claim to have some kind of a short game, Phil is the fellow I most have to thank for it. He's outstanding on the full swing, but on all those little shots from around the green—which is where the game is won or lost most of the time—he is truly a magician.

Phil Rodgers is still pretty much a free spirit in many ways—after all, he's a born-and-bred Southern Californian—so it's taken him a while to get around to putting his knowledge of golf down on paper. If you're serious about the game and really want to play it better, I'm sure as you get into what follows that you will become glad he finally took the time to do so.

I don't know whether his book will becomes a best-seller, but it sure ought to!

Jack Nicklaus
North Palm Beach, Florida
November, 1985

CONTENTS

Foreword by Jack Nicklaus

Section I
THE FULL SWING

1
The Follow-through......19

2
The Backswing and Downswing......23

3
Grip and Address......49

4
The Pitch Shot......67

Section II
PLAYING THE GAME

5
Chipping......81

6
Putting......91

7
The Sand Game......109

8
Shotmaking......133

9
Managing Your Game......138

Introduction

As a teacher of golf I am not a dispenser of Band-Aids. I want my pupils to grow, not just be fixed for a moment. I want them to swing the club in a way that will last a lifetime. You can probably use some of the principles of my teachings such as balance and tempo in the way you now swing the golf club. They will improve your performance, and that's fine. But my intention with this book is to present an overall swing concept in which each element complements all the others.

There are some key words and phrases I use often in my teaching. They include Balance, Underhanded, Overhanded, Light and Heavy, Low to High. These terms will be explained as they apply to how I believe the golf club should be swung, but the explanations will not be very complicated because the terms have universal meanings and sensations. You can put these words into tangible feels. You can *feel* underhandedness, lightness, low to high. This is one good reason why I use such terms. You don't need a special knowledge of golf, or of my swing concepts, to get the sense of them.

This is also why I like to say that I don't teach a system or method, although it will seem that way. "Method" and "system" suggest only one way to produce good golfers. Many golfers have idiosyncrasies, such as Arnold Palmer's blocked hand-action, and turn them into a system. But only Arnold could do what he did, no one else can. I want to emphasize *universal* fundamentals. I think my way is the natural way to play golf because it is based on balance, coordination, freedom from excessive tension. My objective is to get golfers into a position where they must hit the ball with force to make it go straight, yet are not putting abnormal strains on the body. The key to that is having all parts of the swing working as a single unit.

The fundamentals I teach are broken into two categories: Preswing and Swing. I will discuss each element at length but want to set them up for you at this point.

In the Preswing there are:
1. Grip
2. Posture
3. Ball position in relation to left side of the face and right shoulder
4. Hand, arms, clubshaft square to target line
5. Correct tilt of spine
6. Aiming of body and clubface
7. Weight distribution

In the Swing there are:
1. Clubface angle throughout swing (it is

always at right angles to the path of swing)

2. Shaft and clubface always in line with the straight left arm

3. The follow-through always as long, or longer than, the backswing

In a few ways, I go against the grain of much golf instruction that has been disseminated over the years. For example, I believe there has been too much emphasis on keeping the knees flexed and the weight back toward the heels of the feet. Both inhibit flexibility or lightness and quickness of body movement.

I also think that taking the club straight back from the ball and keeping it low to the ground at the start of the swing is wrong. It promotes a disjointed swing, the arms and hands going in one direction, the body in another. That kind of separation makes for inconsistent shotmaking.

My swing concepts are based, in part, on new research into how the body functions. Biomechanics, the scientific study of physical movement, is one such research field. It is having a significant impact on the performance of Olympic athletes, but is also being used increasingly in golf instruction. Many of my concepts are very much in line with, and are supported by, biomechanics. I have used it often in analyzing students. Dr. Ralph Mann is a leading figure in biomechanics, and he has written an excellent rationale for its use in golf:

"The art of properly striking a golf ball with a clubhead that reaches a velocity of over 100 m.p.h. at contact, is one of the most difficult sport skills. Due to the velocities involved, small movement errors can greatly affect the final product (the golf shot), producing frustrating results. The human eye can only distinguish movements of one-fourth of a second or longer to completion. No human eye can actually see what occurs during the impact portion of the swing. In addition, working at a maximum speed, the eye must focus on one small area while totally ignoring all other input."

Thus, biomechanics. A golfer's swing is filmed with a high-speed motion picture camera, from which electronic measurements are made of such things as stresses on various muscles and joints. From these findings suggestions are made on how to swing the club more efficiently.

But biomechanical studies from other sports can also be used in golf. For example, in a study of Olympic champion Carl Lewis, it was found that when he runs only his legs and feet, and arms and hands move. His *upper body and head remain still*. I can relate that to the best use of the upper body in the golf swing.

It is true that the upper body, the back and shoulders, must coil during the backswing. But the *emphasis* should be on coiling the lower body in the backswing. If a golfer's upper body is wound tighter than his lower body, it will naturally unwind first in the downswing. This generally produces erratic golf shots and inconsistent ball striking.

An analogy I often use to express the most efficient body motion in the golf swing is the difference between a metronome and pendulum. The metronome is top-heavy, and an athletic endeavor is seldom done well when the upper body is out of balance. The pendulum represents a lighter, more balanced movement. In golf terms, it is the movement of the lower body. I am a pendulum man. I want the lower body to be the actor and the upper body to be the reactor; the upper body responds to the action of the lower body.

All this is to let you know where I'm coming

from in my teaching. It's my obligation to relay my message without your having to indulge in a guessing game or learn a new terminology. I don't believe in standing above my students and simply expecting to be understood just because I'm the professional.

What and who else has influenced my approach to golf? I started playing when I was 8 years old at a little pitch-and-putt course in San Diego called Presidio Hills. A man there named Al Abrego was a very well-qualified teacher of junior golfers, and he ran an excellent program for kids. He started me in a good direction by stressing an up-and-down swing and keeping in balance.

It was also a good experience playing my first golf on a short course; I didn't play a full-sized course until I was 10. I learned a lot of things about the short game and "touch" shots at Presidio Hills that gave me an advantage over my contemporaries when I began to play in tournaments.

When I started caddieing at La Jolla Country Club and playing there often because my high school golf team was given playing privileges, I came to know Paul Runyan. Paul was then, and still is, one of the best golf teachers in the game. He is especially famous for his short game, and much of what I know in that area stems from Paul's instruction. But he was very important to my development as a golfer in other respects, too.

He taught me how to use my imagination on the golf course, how to improvise. I learned from Paul not only how to hit low and high shots and a variety of chips and pitches, but when to use them in terms of course conditions and competitive circumstances. A small man

physically, throughout his own playing career Paul was constantly searching for ways to overcome his lack of great power. He was a master at course management and gave me an excellent education in how to use the golf course and my skills to the best advantage. I accepted Paul's advice, not merely because he had been a very successful player on the tour, or because I knew from my own experience that he was right, but also because the game became more interesting. Golf can be monotonous if you don't learn to do a lot of little things with the golf ball. It's fun and stimulating to try something new or different.

Paul also tried to influence my life-style as best he could, but there he didn't quite make it. He always said I would destroy myself with my mouth, and not by talking but by eating.

Then there was a man for whom I often caddied and eventually played a lot of golf with, "LoBall" Johnny Wilson. He was a nice golfer and a gambler for high stakes. I'm not ashamed to say that he taught me, from his gambling background, some worthwhile things about playing golf. This may not be the most recommended golf "school" in the world, but it was part of my experience and very useful in a golfing way.

Wilson was a very organized man, and he looked for that characteristic, or the lack of it, in the people he decided to play golf with. When he saw someone who just grabbed a club from his bag and hit a shot without much preparation, Wilson saw someone to bet against. He also observed putting strokes and taught me to be wary of people who swung the putter with a nice pendulum motion. The fellow with the big, long strokes, and the quick jabbers, are the ones most likely to break down under pressure.

Wilson also stressed the importance of the short game in regard to an attitude toward competing. He told me once that the last two shots on every hole are the ones that really count, and I've never forgotten that. I've always played on that basis; which means, never give up on a hole until it is definitely completed. You never know what might happen. The other guy may miss a short putt, and you may get lucky and roll in a long one.

The value of the short game and how to play it were impressed on me from the very beginning of my golf career. But, at the same time, I was developing my theories on the full swing. I have pictures of my swing when I was 10, and can see the positions I now teach. I also helped myself by swinging man-sized clubs at the start. Everyone said they were too big for me, but it was a good thing to do because I had to learn to keep the club, and myself, in balance; that was the only way I could hit the ball. It also made me strong physically and thus a longer hitter than most people my size.

Around the same time, I got to watch Sam Snead play a lot of golf, and he said something to me that has stuck to this day. Referring to a piece of golf technique popular at the time that said that the left heel should stay on the ground throughout the swing, Sam said: "There are a lot of nice golfers who swing from the knees up, but the best play from the *ground* up." In other words, the left heel must rise up during the backswing. That represents playing "from the ground up," using the feet in the swing to produce better rhythm and balance. Sam Snead, of course, had all the balance and rhythm anyone could wish for.

Later, I began to play a lot of golf with Gene Littler. He has been another major influence on my game and how I teach it. I was already pretty much convinced that the golf club must be swung with an even pace from start to finish, but being around Gene left absolutely no doubt. He was, and is, the epitome of the pendulum-type golf swing.

A golf swing should be as tension-free as possible. Central to this is a coordinated movement of all the working parts. It is the same as when you walk. You don't put your left foot out faster than your right foot. Nor do you walk with your arms swinging faster than your legs; the arms swing along at essentially the same

pace. It is just that kind of synchronized movement that makes a good, repeatable golf swing.

Tension is self-inflicted. It sometimes comes from a fear of failure, which translates into attempts to steer a golf ball toward a target. Tension also comes from wanting to hit the ball very hard, and farther than you are actually capable of doing. After you work with my swing concepts I suspect you will hit the ball farther, but everyone has his limits and should recognize and accept them. In most cases, the tensed-up golfer stands flat-footed and with his feet too wide apart. He is stiff-legged, stiff-hipped, stiff-armed. All of which makes it virtually impossible to create a rhythmic, pendulum-type swing. The ball is rarely steered on-target, because taut muscles do not respond very well to high-hope mental signals. And there is not much power developed because tense muscles are not very flexible. Very often the swing is short and quick. That's because the body instinctively does not like tension and wants relief from it as quickly as possible.

I'm a firm believer in such instincts affecting athletic performance, even though mechanical principles are what we tend to think most about. I also believe that all of us have those instincts, that we are better athletes than we tend to give ourselves credit for.

Furthermore, tension produces the worst kind of missed shots. Every golfer does himself a big favor by realizing and accepting the fact that he is not going to hit too many shots perfectly during a round of golf. The great Ben Hogan said that even during his very best rounds he hit only four or five shots just right. Hogan had higher standards than most golfers, but the point is, the better the golfer, the better his mis-hits; they end up closer to the target and

in less trouble than the mis-hits of poorer players.

Golf is not a game of great shots, it's a game of great misses.

You rarely see golfers hit exceptionally poor shots who have a flowing, well-coordinated swing. They usually hit the ball with considerable power, too. Many people mistake tension for a feeling of strength and control. But true strength and control come from coordination.

Many golf teachers advise taking the club back slowly, then increasing the speed of the swing on the downswing. I don't think that's the right way to play. An uneven tempo creates abnormal tension. Backswing tempo, or pace, should be natural to the individual and matched by an equally natural downswing speed. Sam Snead in his prime was one of the longest hitters in golf, yet there was never the sense that he was *hitting* the ball because the tempo of his entire swing was so perfectly balanced.

Even relatively faster swingers, such as Tom Watson, Arnold Palmer, Lanny Wadkins and Ben Hogan, are very effective because they are "fast" back and through; in other words, evenly paced. Rhythm doesn't have to do with speed as much as it does with synchronization, coordination, balance. I can't stress that too much. It applies to every phase of the game, from driving a ball 250 yards to rolling a putt two feet.

On Balance

It should be obvious by now that balance plays a very important role in my whole concept of the golf swing. Because it does, I want to expand further on the subject at this early stage of the book.

Balance means always being stable on the

ground, as the movement of the body and club progresses from the beginning to the end of the golf swing. Granted, Gary Player seems to lose his balance on some of his long shots, but I don't see it as that. Gary's a small man who feels he must extend his body with a maximum effort. He does this with a terrific amount of energy, and having extended himself to the absolute limit, his falling out of balance is a result of centrifugal force. But he is always falling, or walking, forward after these swings. All his energy is going toward the target. He never falls backward. This means to me that he is on balance during the most crucial parts of his swing—before, during and well beyond impact.

You have control of your swing when you are in balance. Only when you and your swing are in balance will the path of the club be repeated consistently. Golfers who are in balance hit more shots the same way than those who are not in balance. They put the ball through the same "hole" in the air time after time.

Balance itself is not a mechanic. It is the result of certain body positions and movements that follow Newton's law of physics that for every action there is an equal and opposite reaction. The essence of it is *balance.*

Balance, as I apply it to the golf swing, is expressed by certain essential positions and movements. For example, the angle of the club is identical at particular key points in the swing. You don't hit the ball with one side of the body or the other dominating; you hit it with both sides of the body. And the body should turn an equal amount on both sides of the swing. Ideally, the body turns 90 degrees from the address position on the backswing. Thus, it should turn at least 90 degrees on the downswing and through-swing.

The 'look' of my swing

There are certain overriding characteristics to the swing I teach. They are fairly easy to recognize because they are probably not what you usually see. I will point them out here briefly, to give you an overall picture of what to expect through the rest of this book. I think it's important to have this kind of view early on, so the details I develop as we go along will be more meaningful.

For one thing, the clubhead rises up off the ground rather soon. It does not come straight up, but neither does it ride low to the ground at the start of the backswing.

For another thing, the swing path of the *whole* club is more inside to out than parallel. The club moves in toward the body then away from it on the backswing and in on the downswing and away from it on the forward swing. The arms swing up over the right and left shoulders; it's a V-shaped swing.

I feel strongly that the inside-to-out swing is more effective than any other. If you err it should be on the inside-to-out path; which is to say, you can hardly swing too much inside to out. Most golfers swing the club from outside to in, which is why they slice the ball a lot or pull it far to the left of the target. My goal is to get everyone hitting his shots from right to left in the air—hooking, or drawing (which is a mild hook). The hook or draw is a stronger and essentially more natural shot than the slice, or fade (which is a mild slice). If you learn to hook the ball, then you can become a straight-ball hitter, which is the ultimate.

With my concept, you will hit the ball as though you were tossing it underhanded. The feeling is one of hitting under the ball and then up. The object is to keep the head of the club going at the target as long as possible. When golfers swing the club from outside to in, they're swinging as though they were throwing it overhanded like a baseball pitcher or like someone chopping logs. It's not as effective as swinging underhanded, the club going from low to high, which helps you start the ball to the right and draw it left back to the target.

Teaching priorities

Every golf teacher with a concept for swinging the club has an order of importance in teaching it. I begin at the end, teaching the follow-through first. I do this because I believe that when you know where you want to be at the end of a swing *before* you begin it, you are more inclined to do all that is necessary to reach your goal. It's like reading a road map before starting a trip. You find your destination, then trace back to the starting point. Invariably, you find the most efficient route and avoid troublesome detours and backtracking. Put it this way, golfers rarely play as well to blind targets as they do to those they can see all the way. And how do you appraise an upcoming golf shot? You look first at the target, then follow the terrain back to your ball.

From the follow-through I go to the backswing and downswing, then to the grip and address. Afterward there is an extensive section on shotmaking, managing your game, how to practice and take a lesson.

Naturally, all facets of the golf swing are meant to be integrated into a single, coordinated action. But in book form each must be considered separately. However, I will bring the various elements together at the end of the chapters, with sequence photographs to provide an overall context.

Phil Rodgers

The Follow-through

The follow-through of your golf swing should reflect the positions taken and movements you've executed during the backswing. In many cases there is an almost exact reversal or mirror image.

Listed below are the key positions to be in at the completion of the golf swing as I teach it, along with photographs illustrating their mirror images in the backswing. Aside from the specific positions, your objective in the follow-through is to finish every swing with the club under control and your body in balance. I have never seen a poor shot result when a golfer has met these criteria.

No. 1—Here are the key follow-through positions.

The upper body has rotated 90 degrees to the left of the address position, and the club is at a 90-degree angle to the straightened right arm.

The club is over the left shoulder, just where it would be on a *left-hander's backswing*.

(As indicated by the picture, the body turn actually goes somewhat beyond 90-degrees, and the club goes farther to complete the follow-through, as a reaction to letting the shaft release at the end of the swing.)

The chest is facing directly at the target. The left leg is straight and carries approximately 85 percent of the body weight, or 30 percent more than at address—weight distribution at address favors the left side at a ratio of about 55-45; it is more to the left with short shots such as pitches and chips.

The mirror image: In the backswing the upper body has rotated 90 degrees, and the club is at a 90-degree angle to the straight left arm. The club is over the right shoulder.

The chest is facing directly away from the target. The right leg is virtually straight and carries approximately 75 percent of the body weight or 30 percent more than at address.

Generally, when the weight transfer is equal —30 percent to the right, 30 percent to the left—the ball will hook, or draw, in flight. If the

weight transfer is less than equal, the ball will slice to the right.

No. 2—The left side of the body is taller, or longer, than the right side. The left shoulder is higher than the right shoulder. The right side is curved inward.

The right arm is fully extended. The left arm is folded so its elbow points to the ground, indicating a release of tension.

The butt of the club is pointing at the target. Both thumbs are directly under the handle of the club and supporting it. (Both positions are at the very end of the follow-through—see insert photographs.)

The mirror image: On the backswing, the right side is longer than the left side. The right shoulder is higher than the left shoulder. The left side is curved inward.

The left arm is fully extended. The right arm is folded so its elbow points to the ground.

The butt of the club is pointed directly away from the target, and both thumbs are under the handle of the club to support it. (Both positions are at the very end of the backswing—see insert photographs.)

No. 3—The right knee is pointing directly at the target. The right foot is raised so its sole faces directly away from the target; all 11 spikes are showing.

The mirror image: On the backswing the left knee is behind the ball and pointing directly away from the target.

(On the backswing the left foot does not rise nearly as high as the right foot does on the follow-through. However, it is important that the right foot get into the position indicated above for the follow-through.)

Keep in mind that a golf swing is not over the moment after you've hit the ball. Although the ball is very quickly off the clubface, if you think this way you will almost invariably slow the swing *before* impact. This is often caused by tension. Or more tension is created when you try to slow the club down. A simple experiment will prove that to you: Stop a downswing abruptly and feel how taut your arms and hands become.

Swinging through is, in effect, a relaxation of tension in the left arm and hand, and a building of positive tension in the right arm, hand and side that is the result of centrifugal force.

Your goal is not so much to hit the ball but to reach the follow-through positions. The ball has merely gotten in the way of the club as it travels into the follow-through.

The Backswing and Downswing

An overview

Two basic reference points must be established at this time because they are referred to frequently in discussing the golf swing. They are two imaginary lines.

One line runs from the target back to and beyond the center of the golf ball. It is called the "target line." The clubhead rests on this line at address and swings along it through the impact area. This area is referred to as the "flat spot."

A second imaginary line runs parallel to the target line. It is called the "parallel line." Your feet touch up to this line at address so that they and your body are aimed on a parallel line to the left of the target.

With feet and clubhead, respectively, square to the parallel and target lines, backswing begins with a gradual up-cocking of the hands and turning of entire upper body so club swings simultaneously up and in.

Clubhead has quickly gotten above butt of club by pushing down with left and lifting with the right hand so it is under control of golfer.

Butt-end of club and hands remain as low as possible for as long as possible to get maximum extension of left arm.

There has been no rotation of clubface as backswing is completed. Shoulders have remained at a right angle to the spine throughout the backswing.

In downswing, club follows almost same path it took on backswing. Wrists begin to uncock early, but clubhead stays above hands until hands have reached lowest point in swing.

Club has moved from inside to square at impact. Hands are as low as possible, in identical position as at address.

The path of the swing is controlled by the arms, hands and butt-end of club—the hands and butt being virtually a single unit.

Palm of the right hand, and clubface, are at 90-degree angles to target and parallel lines. Right shoulder has worked "under" so club swings up and out toward target. Shape of entire swing is a V.

Swinging the WHOLE club

The path of the whole club during the swing controls the initial direction of the ball's flight. Ideally, that direction is straight at the target.

The position of the clubface in relation to the path of the club controls the spin of the ball and therefore also affects its trajectory. The correct position is a 90-degree or right angle to the swing path. That angle is often referred to as "square." If the clubface is square when it contacts the ball, the ball will have perfect underspin and fly straight or with a little curve to the left.

The idea is to set the clubface square at address, and make sure *the angle does not change during the course of the swing.* If the angle changes, if there is any rotation of the clubface at any time in the backswing, it must somehow be manipulated in the downswing so it is square at impact. Such manipulation is possible, but it is difficult to do consistently. One time the clubface may be "closed"—aimed to the left when it strikes the ball—another time it may be "open"—aimed to the right.

I want to avoid such manipulation. A central feature of my swing concept is the elimination of clubface rotation during the swing through a gradual up-cocking of the wrists on the backswing; it is a lever effect in which the left hand pushes down and the right hand lifts up. I will describe that action in much greater detail in a few moments, and say here only that it avoids even the *idea* of playing golf entirely with the clubface.

I want you to play with the notion that the golf ball is hit with the *whole* club. An image I like to use to project that idea is a swinging door. The whole door (club) swings open and shut. The door hinge (your spine) is the axis on which the door swings.

The shape of the swing

The path of the swing is controlled by the arms, hands and butt of the club—the hands and butt being virtually a single unit. The path is essentially inside to out. Most golf instruction relates that to the target line. I prefer relating it to the golfer's body. I believe this makes it easier to perceive. The arms, hands and butt of the club move in toward the body on the backswing, stay close to it on the downswing and go away from it on the through-swing.

The general *sense* of the swing path I want you to have is inside to out. In fact, the total

The spine is the axis of the swing and must only rotate in place during the swing.

swing path of the club, in relation to the target line, is inside to out to square (then back to inside in the follow-through).

In effect, the total swing path is inside to out to *square* (to inside). However, I will refer to it as inside to out throughout this book, because that is the *sense* of the path I want you to have.

The arc of the swing

An integral part of the swing path is the arc, which is the circular movement of the club in relation to your spine. It is the up-and-down (and up) part. It has nothing to do with the target. The plane of the swing does. It is the

parallel part, the club swinging more or less parallel to the ground.

The hands and butt of the club, and the clubhead, each make a circle. The less they deviate from their circular motions, the more consistent your shotmaking will be!

Another measure of the quality of the swing is the distance the butt of the club is from the ball at the top of the backswing, compared with the clubhead. I want *the butt to be as far or farther away than the clubhead*. The farther away it is, the more power and control you will have. The key to this is keeping the hands and butt as low as possible for as long as you can. This pro-

Indication that there has been no side-to-side or lateral movement of spine is that the distances of the head and hips from the ball do not change from what they were at address until the ball is away and you are into the follow-through.

Examples of two common swing faults. The reverse pivot. Weight stays on left side in backswing. Spine tilts left, along with the left shoulder; in downswing, weight shifts to right foot—a fall-back-and-fire action that invariably produces weak, poorly directed shots.

motes extension of the left arm and a full and complete turn of the hips and shoulders.

The axis

I want as little side-to-side movement of the body as possible. The key to creating this compact and controlled movement is the axis on which it is made. That axis is the golfer's spine, which should never move in any direction. That is, the spine rotates *in place* as the arms swing and the shoulders and hips turn. The more stationary is the spine as it rotates, the more consistent is the swing.

There is a method I use to determine how well the spine (axis) is functioning in the swing. At address, certain distances and angles are established; the hips and head are so far from the ball, for example, and the right shoulder is a little lower than the left shoulder. When you return to impact with the ball, those distances and angles—with the exception of the hips—should be as close as possible to what they were at address.

The gear concept

The coordinated movement of all the body parts, and the club, can be put in the context of gears. There are three: the body, the arms and hands, and the club. All are attached more or less to the axis. Although some people's arms are longer than those of others, and the clubs are of different lengths, for the sake of simplicity I'm going to consider that everyone's "gears" are the same size and length.

The sway. Instead of a turn, the dominant move is a slide to the right so right side is past the right foot. This movement of the body promotes a sideways move in the opposite direction. The sliding action is difficult to time correctly, so accuracy and power of shots are erratic.

Now, let's say the body is a one-inch gear, being closest to the axis point—the spine—and will make the smallest circle as it turns. The arms and hands, an extension of the body, are a two-inch gear. The club, an extension of the arms, is a four-inch gear. The rate of speed at which each gear turns should be in proportion to its size relative to the other gears and its distance from the axis. Thus, if the body turns at five m.p.h., say, the arms must swing 10 m.p.h., and the club 20 m.p.h. If one gear moves proportionately slower than the other two, the swing is not synchronized.

The tendency is for the longest gear (the club) to be slower than the other two. This is why golfers slice, especially with the driver, because as the club gets longer it must move faster to cover a greater distance in proportion to the other gears. It is important that the longest, or outside, gear always goes fast enough. The faster it goes, the faster the two inside gears can go.

When I discuss the so-called "late hit," I will refer back to the gear concept.

The sequence of moves

You want to *feel* that your whole body and the club operate as a single unit throughout the entire swing, with no part moving independently of any of the others. That's the ideal.

In fact, in order to keep the club on the correct swing path, certain body parts must move sooner, or later, than others. The space between each of these movements is almost infinitesimal. To the naked eye it is as though all the parts move as a piece and, as I say, it should *feel* that way, too. Still, there is a sequence.

The backswing begins with the swing of the arms and hands, then a turning of the shoulders and hips, followed by the movement of the legs and feet.

In the *downswing,* that sequence is exactly the opposite. It starts with the feet, and the raised left heel hitting the ground as though it were driving a nail. Then the legs move, followed by the turning of the hips and shoulders and a swinging of the arms and hands.

Both the backswing and downswing are done in the same rhythm; it is one-two, one-two.

It is very important that the arms and hands do not move first in the downswing. This almost in- variably produces an overhand-toss motion that can sling the clubhead out beyond the target line and well away from the body. It must then move back toward the body to get to the ball. That's an outside-to-in swing path, the one that produces the most inconsistent, erratic ball striking. When done correctly, the hips and arms are actually pulled by the turn of the hips into the transition, or change of direction, from the backswing to the downswing.

At no time do you ever swing *only* the club or clubhead. They swing because the arms and hands do and because the body turns. The ultimate golf shot is struck with no conscious control of the club. Remember, the body rotates the arms swing back and forth, the wrists swing up and down.

The Backswing

The clubhead, the heaviest part of the club, is on the ground at address. The grip, the lightest part, is above it. I want that distribution changed as smoothly and as soon as possible. I want the clubhead above the grip so the arms and hands are in control of the swing—not the clubhead.

The wrists/hands as a lever

That redistribution begins at the start of the backswing, when *the wrists and hands cock upward*. The up-cocking is in conjunction with the swing of the arms and the turn of the shoulders.

It continues until there is a 90-degree angle between the golf club and the left arm. The arm swing and shoulder turn take the club the rest of the way in the backswing.

No lifting

Only the up-cocking of the wrists/hands raises the clubhead. The arms, hands, and butt of the club, as a unit, should move parallel to the ground until clearly past the right leg.

There must be no lifting of the club with the arms in the first 12 to 16 inches of the backswing. If the arms do any lifting, the handle will come up and not let the clubhead come up quickly enough.

With the up-cocking action you will feel as if the butt of the club is being pushed downward. In fact, you can do just that. Depress the butt, and raise the clubhead as the backswing begins. Think *handle low, clubhead high!*

As a practice drill to get the feel of the up-cocking action, I have students hit balls with that as the first move. The wrists/hands cock up until a 90-degree angle has been created by the club and the underside of the left arm. Then the arms swing and the body turns. You'll be surprised how well the ball can be hit this way.

When you do this exercise correctly you should feel a stretching tension in the underside muscles of the left arm and in the left hand. This is a positive tension that you want to keep throughout the backswing. If you lose that tension, you've lost control of the club—the clubhead will drop down.

As I said earlier, the up-cocking, lever action of the wrists/hands makes it almost impossible to rotate the clubface out of its original position at address; it will remain square to the path of the swing. Also, there is far less chance of a variation in the swing path. And there is more control over swing speed, because the arms are swinging the club and an arm swing is more constant than a hands swing.

A golf club weighs roughly a pound, but

when you swing it at 100 m.p.h. the clubhead acts like a 100-pound weight. By up-cocking, and keeping the heavier clubhead above the handle, the clubhead is effectively lighter and the handle has more weight. Thus, it is *the golfer that controls the leverage,* not the clubhead!

The turn takes club inside

The butt of the club "rides" the parallel-to-the-ground line as long as possible at the start of the backswing, as the shoulders and hips turn. As the rotation of the shoulders and hips increases, the arms and hands follow the rotation and bring the club back toward the body. The arms never go farther away from the body than they were at address and may even be closer in the first part of the backswing. (Only with their final extension to complete the backswing, do the arms move away from the body.)

It is a pure turn—rotation with *as little lateral slide as possible.* Weight is transferred toward the right heel, and the right knee tends to straighten—not move laterally. The right side moves farther away from the ball. I use a wall image in teaching this turn.

Imagine a wall only a few inches in front of your body. When the weight transfers from the ball of the right foot toward its heel, and the right knee straightens, the entire right side is moved away from the wall. If it isn't moved "out of the way," the left side will turn into the wall.

The idea is for the right side to move away from the wall so the left side can move *along the wall.*

At start of backswing, arms, hands and butt of club move as a unit parallel to the ground until they are past the right leg. Weight is transferred to the right heel to prevent a sway. The hands and arms follow the rotation of the shoulders and hips and turn continues.

In effect, *the body never gets closer to the golf ball than it was at address!*

The swing path is essentially dictated by the turn of the body. The arms and club swing up and down in front of your body, as it turns to the right and to the left.

Think of it this way: BASICALLY, THE CLUB IS ALWAYS IN FRONT OF YOUR BODY. IT NEVER GETS OUTSIDE THE SHOULDERS AT ANY TIME IN THE SWING.

Or turn the 'triangle'

Another "frame" can be used to illustrate how the club stays in front of the body throughout the swing.

At address your chest, arms and hands form a triangle. The club bisects it. (See illustrations.)

THE TRIANGLE IS RETAINED, and THE CLUB REMAINS WITHIN ITS FRAMEWORK THROUGHOUT THE ENTIRE SWING.

The triangle supports the club, in balance, at both ends of the swing. The club is not "laid off"—it doesn't fall to one side or the other. The shaft is at right angles to the shoulders and supported evenly by both arms and hands.

Elbows keep their distance

So the arms can swing fully back and up, the right arm gradually folds during the backswing but never gets farther away from the left elbow than it was at address.

This type of folding is natural, and most golfers do it instinctively. However, there are some golfers who fold the right elbow so it

The mark of a proper turn is that the body never gets closer to the ball than it was at address. Only with the final extension of the arms to complete the backswing, do the arms move away from the body.

The left heel must be raised off the ground to make a complete turn of the upper body, and left knee cocks to right.

The downswing begins with the left heel dropping to the ground. This assures a proper transfer of weight to the left.

points behind them. This is known as the "flying right elbow." It is not recommended. It causes the "triangle" to change its proportions. The elbows should stay the same distance apart throughout the swing.

Left heel up, left knee to the right

Another aid to making a complete turn of the upper body and hips is to raise the left heel so only the forward third of the foot is on the ground (see illustration). The foot does not go straight up onto its toes. You should feel some pressure on the right-front pad of the foot.

There will be less raising of the left foot when swinging the shorter irons, but there should be some movement. In any case, let it happen. Everyone needs some foot motion. It controls the pace and rhythm of the swing, aids balance and making full turns.

At the same time, *the left knee cocks to the right and slightly behind the ball.*

The bigger the swing, the more motion of the left knee. But in general, the turn of the left knee (and the right knee) should match the turn of the hips—45 degrees.

The weight transfer—from light to heavy

As the backswing develops you will feel the left side of your body getting lighter and the right side getting heavier. This is the effect of a proper transfer of weight *toward the heel of the right foot.*

You should also feel your right side getting farther away from the target line. Pressure will gradually build on *the inside of the right heel.* The right foot should never roll over onto its outer edge.

The head—does it move?

One of golf's oldest instructional adages is "Don't move your head!" It's true, but to consciously try to keep it still breeds tension in the upper body.

In fact, the head will *rotate* with the turn of the shoulders. But, if your posture is correct—the spine, neck and head in a straight line —and the hips, legs and feet move properly, your head will be stable. To repeat, the upper body is the reactor, not the actor, and the head is attached to the upper body. Thus, if the upper body moves improperly, so will the head. That is, the *less you move your feet, legs and hips, the more your upper body and head will move.*

The head should *rotate and remain on a line between your legs* for the entire swing.

"Keep your head down!" is another way of saying don't move the head. But the interpretation of this can be counterproductive. If you try to keep your head down, you may drop it lower than it was at address. Then, to achieve balance, you will raise the head in the downswing. When you raise your head in the downswing, the club will rise up with it. The result: you catch only the top part of the ball and send it low along the ground.

THE HEAD MUST NEVER MOVE UP AND DOWN DURING THE SWING.

You want your head to maintain the same distance from the ball throughout the swing.

When I was a junior golfer, my teacher, Al Abrego, used a drill for learning head movement. A pencil is attached to the bill of your cap and aimed at the ball. If you see the pencil move when you swing, you've moved your head improperly. It's a simple but effective drill.

The Downswing

Underhand it

When you hit the ball, I want you to feel you are tossing it underhanded. Compared with throwing a ball overhanded, the underhand toss is the simpler, more natural physical movement. It is quite accurate, too; you kind of lay the ball out there where you want it to be.

How do you throw a ball underhanded? You raise your throwing arm behind you, then swing it down low, release the ball at the bottom of the swing arc and then let the arm swing up to follow directly behind the flying ball. The arm swings along the target line, then up.

The golf swing I teach is just that, with the golf club an extension of the throwing arm.

What are the mechanics of the underhand toss of the golf club? I have already got your "throwing arm" up and behind you—you are at

In downswing, left hip never slides past ball. Dropping of left heel to ground initiates the action, which straightens left leg. As club moves to impact you want to feel your body is standing tall.

By simultaneously straightening left leg and turning left side, right side automatically moves into underhanded-toss position. The club travels at least 180 degrees during the swing between the top-right and bottom-right pictures.

Hands begin uncocking well before impact.

Wrists recock very soon after impact.

the top of your backswing. Let's take it from there.

Hitting in the 'flat spot'

The goal in the downswing is to have the *clubhead moving parallel to the ground and at the target when the ball is struck* and continuing parallel past the point of impact. That parallel zone is called the "flat spot."

Hitting in the flat spot produces maximum clubhead speed at impact and the greatest control of the shot direction. Most people hit the ball before reaching maximum clubhead speed, because the club is still going down at impact without a full extension of the arms. The more exaggerated is the underhand-toss motion, the farther behind the ball does the flat spot begin.

Also, by hitting in the flat spot, there is not the kind of resistance to the passage of the club that occurs when hitting down on the ball. I don't believe in consciously hitting down on the ball with a full swing.

Hitting in the flat spot is a fundamental feature of my swing concept. But before discussing it at length, I want to talk about other key elements in the downswing.

Down and under, inside to out

The inside-to-out swing path is created to a large extent by the steady straightening of the left leg and turning of the left side. These moves also promote the underhand-toss motion, a "tall" left side and lower, concave right side at impact. (See illustration.)

Remember, the sequence of movements to initiate the downswing begins with the lower body. The uncoiling is "fired" by dropping the raised left foot onto its heel. This starts the weight transfer, which is almost complete

Other moves, other feels

There are other moves that occur in the underhand-toss/inside-to-out downswing. They project certain feelings you should be aware of; use them as checkpoints, or concentrate on them to create the basic swing path.

For example, when you're swinging inside to out and underhanded, it will seem or feel as if the butt of the club drops down. In fact, it is going down but simultaneously moving toward the parallel line. The butt of the club and your hands will pass very close to your right thigh, almost brushing against it.

A home-run hitter in baseball also swings underhanded. If he didn't he wouldn't hit many homers—only ground balls. I tell my students to feel that they're swinging up to the ball. I want them to visualize a three-foot wall about four or five feet in front of them, then try to hit the ball over that wall. You do that by working the club underneath the ball to get it up.

Your right elbow will be very close to your right side . . . snug against it . . . as soon as possible after the start of the downswing. You never want your arms moving up and out. You want them going *down and in,* then up and out. You should feel that you're swinging your arms as close to your right side as possible.

And your right shoulder will be low *and behind the ball.* You want to get the right shoulder under, or low, as soon as possible. The left side is long, the right side is short.

These are the movements, and feels, associated with the inside-to-out/underhand-toss swing.

before the left leg straightens. You want to feel a very distinct straightening of the left knee through impact. I hesitate to use the word lock, but the knee comes very close to that.

The left hip turns away from the ball most effectively when the left leg straightens.

THE LEFT HIP NEVER SLIDES PAST THE BALL.

This straightening and turning action automatically drops the right side into the underhand-toss position. And when you go underhand, you must also go inside to out with the club; it is essentially an automatic response.

The club is already well inside because of the rotation of the body in the backswing. The underhand-toss motion helps to keep the inside-to-out angle.

Getting the clubhead to the ball

Obviously you can't maintain this extreme inside-to-out swing path all the way to impact or you'll hit the ball far to the right of your target. The whole club, the shaft as well as the face, must be square to the target at impact.

Here again, the straightening of the left leg and turning of the left side are the prime moves. The turning, in particular, pulls the arms and butt of the club toward the parallel line. As the turn continues, the arms and butt move onto the line and along it to and through impact (see illustration).

But the hands also play a role in this action.

Hands hit early

At the completion of the backswing the clubhead is above the hands (and handle) and must get below them to strike the ball. This begins to develop at the very start of the downswing. The hands start uncocking at the same time that they begin moving downward from the top of the backswing. *However, the uncocking is not a conscious effort.* The club is not "thrown" at the ball. The hands uncock gradually as a natural result of the left side turning, the folded right arm straightening and the centrifugal force developed by the swinging action.

When the butt of the club reaches the parallel line, the clubhead is still slightly above the handle (see illustration). Only when the shaft is parallel to the target line and the ground, *and the hands are at their lowest point in the swing,* does the clubhead drop below the handle onto the target line and into the flat spot. The ball is then struck.

The main objective is to get the hands and club as low as you can, as soon as you can. Then all the other things can happen, including a *relaxation of tension in the left arm and hand after impact and on the follow-through.* You want

to make the club go from behind you to in front of you, and the right hand and arm going toward the target, as soon as possible in the swing. The sooner you get the club pointing to the target, the less tension there is in the left shoulder, left arm and hand. The clubhead wants to get up quickly after impact and have maximum extension toward the target.

The positions at impact

At the moment of impact with the ball, the clubface and both hands are at 90-degree angles to the target line and parallel line, respectively. The palm of the right hand and the back of the left hand are facing the target (see illustration).

The left arm and club are fully extended, and the inside of the left shoulder and arm, and the shaft form a single unbroken unit on an exact line with the back of the ball.

The wrists have completely uncocked so the club is swinging at full speed. The chest is directly facing the ball. The chest and arms form the triangle described earlier.

The hands recock

I want the right hand and arm above the left as soon as possible after impact. This, in effect, is a continuation of the uncocking action begun at the start of the downswing and constitutes a recocking of the wrists/hands. The heavy end of the club is once again above the light end and very quickly so.

The left elbow will fold into the same position the right elbow took on the backswing. This is a result of the relaxation, or release of tension, in the left arm.

When the hands are just above waist high, the club and fully-extended right arm point to the target; the shaft points up. You create a right angle between the underside of the left forearm and the shaft, which mirrors the position of the shaft and right forearm at the same point in the backswing (see illustration).

The club then swings around your body and up over your left shoulder and behind your head to complete the total swing. The shaft is now above your arms, and the toe of the club points directly *toward* the target area; *the toe never points toward the ground.*

As I stressed in the chapter on the follow-through, when you know where the club, your hands and arms, etc., are supposed to be after the ball is struck, you will do what must be done before impact to make good contact.

The recocking of the hands immediately after impact insures that you do not slow them down through impact. You want to keep the speed up as long as possible.

Better early than late

Many golfers make a conscious effort to *not* uncock their hands on the downswing until the last possible instant. They are trying to prevent a hook by "hanging on" with the left hand. This is also known as the "late hit," or "saving your hit." You want a gradual, smooth acceleration.

Recalling the three-gear concept, when going for a late hit you are, in effect, moving the third gear—the club—proportionately slower than the other two through the total downswing. If it continues at that ratio, with the arms and body going faster, the club will never get to square at impact. At impact the hands and arms must slow down to let the club catch up. The club then explodes by the ball and creates a "snap hook," the ball diving sharply down and to the left.

If the club doesn't catch up, the ball is pushed or sliced to the right, because the body turns too quickly and pulls the hands and club across the ball from outside to in.

To avoid the slice or push, the body must stop turning to let the club catch up. Or the club must be sped up to synchronize with the other two gears. But there is hardly time. It takes tremendously strong wrists to bring the heaviest part of the club into correct alignment for impact with the ball. The players who make a career in long-driving contests can do it. But they are also, generally, very wild off the tee.

The clubhead's speed at impact is much quicker when it is not retarding the swing by being below the hands. The clubhead wants to drop because it is heavy, and you must resist it doing so throughout most of the swing. You don't want to keep the clubhead back, as in the late hit, you want to keep it up; the toe of the club should be higher than the heel as long as possible.

The late hit can create a powerful shot, but not powerful enough to make up for the inconsistency it brings to the game. It is extremely difficult to time.

The idea is to have a smooth transition from the backswing to the downswing. The ball is hit straighter and with maximum power when the body, arms and hands, and club move with constant acceleration in proportion to their size throughout the entire swing.

For another thing, the late hit makes the shaft of the club flex too much. The holding back of the club creates a tremendous bowing of the shaft, and *the best golf is played with the least amount of shaft flex.*

That statement may come as a surprise, which is why it is emphasized. Most golfers believe that the more the shaft flexes, the farther the ball goes. But the primary function of flex in the golf shaft is to get the ball up in the air.

Every golfer needs some shaft flex, but it is always an unpredictable element and the more it can be minimized the better off you are. By way of exaggeration, it doesn't take too many swings of a club with a soft rubber shaft to realize the ball doesn't go very far when hit. This also illustrates how important it is for the body and arms to swing proportionately slower than the club.

Which gets back to how, and why, the hands should start uncocking at the start of the downswing. It is a gradual and natural action that is coordinated with the swing of the arms and turn of the body. There is no sudden flick of the hands. There is a smooth, even acceleration of the club.

In fact, more power is generated because it is a coordinated effort. Three power elements working together in a swing are going to make a stronger hit than if only one is involved. Slapping a door shut—the equivalent of a late hit—is never as powerful as slamming it closed with the hands, arms and body working as a single unit. It doesn't even feel as though you've hit the door. It seems light and effortless, just as it does when we hit our best golf shots. It's why Sam Snead, who was called "The Slammer," never looked like he was hitting the ball as far as he did.

The 'flat spot'

For years golfers have been told to "hit down" on the ball with their irons. It seems logical. How else do you get it airborne? But hitting down means the club continues downward into the ground after impact. I want something different. I am very much opposed to "hitting down." *I want to hit under the ball, and up.* That's the feeling when you are hitting in the flat spot.

I want the club moving parallel, or level, with the ground when it strikes the ball, and continuing level for some five or six inches afterward. The parallel zone, as I said earlier, is the flat spot.

With irons, the flat spot begins at the bottom of the ball. In other words, the club is on a descending plane when it gets to the *back of the ball,* but the plane is very shallow at this point and the clubhead will be in the flat spot when it gets directly under the ball.

With the fairway woods, the ball is hit in the middle of the flat spot.

With the driver, when the ball is up on a tee, the ball is hit in the last half of the flat spot. That is to say, the clubhead will be traveling parallel to the ground for three to five inches *before* it strikes the ball. You never want the driver descending at impact.

A slicer has little or no flat spot, and a hooker's flat spot is too far behind the ball. Flat-spot length varies with the ability to create the underhanded swing. The more underhanded you are, the longer is your effective flat spot.

The natural flat spot starts at the left side of your face and ends just about at the end of your left shoulder. This can be set up in the address position. With the driver, your face is two inches behind the ball. With the irons, the left side of your face is on a line with the back of the ball.

(Left) Clubhead nears "flat spot" zone well behind ball, because of early uncocking of wrists. At impact (right), with driver, clubhead has traveled some five inches in the zone. The clubhead must never be in a descending attitude at impact.

Advantages in the 'flat spot'

An important advantage to hitting in the flat spot is less resistance to the clubhead. The clubhead will be low enough to strike the ball flush and get it properly airborne, but not so low that the ground will slow its progress into the follow-through. The clubhead moves more quickly through impact, and shots are stronger and more consistent. It also eliminates the "flyer," the shot that jumps very quickly off the clubface with no controlling spin and goes much farther than it should.

On the other hand, when "hitting down" the clubhead may not be stopped, but it will *always be slowed.*

Then, too, when "hitting down" the ball tends to jump too quickly off the clubface if the grass is loose, and roll up the clubface off tight grass. It is more of a glancing blow. It may seem solid, but the ball is not being fully compressed because it doesn't stay long enough on the face of the club. The longer the ball stays on the clubface, the greater the compression. More compression translates into more power and control.

The ball stays on the clubface longer when hitting in the flat spot, because the clubface moves with the ball upon impact. It is a level blow like a straight punch. I realize the ball may stay on the clubface only the briefest instant longer, but every instant counts. Again I use the image of the slammed door compared with the door that is slapped shut.

The best indication you've hit in the flat spot is the divot that is taken. It will be the same depth throughout, not any deeper at one point

(Left) Ball is away, but clubhead is still in "flat spot" zone and following directly behind ball. Ball has been "slammed" with square face, and full force, of club, which begins to rise only when well past impact.

than at another. And it will be a shallow divot, sometimes just shreds of grass, because the clubhead only grazes the top of the ground. No great hunks of turf go flying as when "hitting down."

Shock reduction

Another advantage to hitting in the flat spot is less shock to the hands and arms. I believe a lot of golfers are not as good as they could be with the irons because they instinctively fear the sting or shock that can come from an iron club banging sharply into the ground. As a result, they tend to tense up before impact, which causes the club to slow down.

When you hit in the flat spot the feeling is of lightness and of no effort.

Grip and Address

E verything I say here about the grip and address is aimed at facilitating the kind of golf swing I teach. Naturally.

The Grip

The 'neutral' grip. Hands not twisted right or left minimizes grip's influences on swing-path and angle of clubface at impact.

Hands in 'neutral'

I refer to the grip I recommend as being in "neutral." Most golfers turn their hands in one direction or the other on the handle. I prefer very little turning so that the grip's influence on the swing path and clubface is minimized and, also, to reduce tension.

For example, the majority of golfers turn the left hand to the right on the handle (see illustration). This position tends to build tension in the back of the left wrist. It also creates a kind of cupping motion with the left hand at the start of the backswing that can change the alignment of the clubface.

With the grip I teach, there is only a slight kink, or "cup," formed where the back of each hand joins its wrist. This is a natural result of how the hands are set at address.

The left-hand hold

To take the grip with the left hand, set the handle along the calluses. I don't want the club to be held any more in the fingers than in the palm. You should be able to make a good fist with the left hand.

To complete the left-hand grip, curl all four fingers around the handle and *set the pad of the hand on top of it.*

Many golfers set the thumb slightly to the right of center on the top of the handle. I want the thumb running down the very center of it to promote maximum strength and club control.

A lot of grip instruction talks about the golfer being able to see a certain number of knuckles of the left hand when looking from the address position. But that should not be a measure of a grip. Everyone's grip is going to look a little different, owing to individual hand-size. The important thing is to *get the correct-size grips on your clubs.* A grip is the correct size when the left hand closes around the handle and the tips of all the fingers just barely touch the pad of the hand.

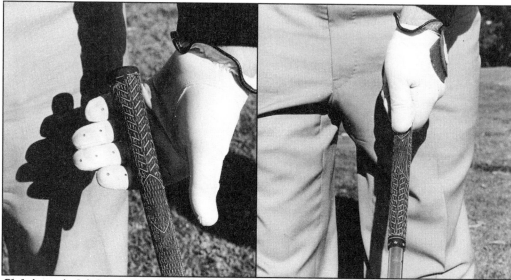

Club is set in left hand along line where fingers connect with palm. Club is not held any more in fingers than in palm.

Curl fingers around handle, and set thumb down very center of grip for maximum strength and club control.

The right-hand connection

There are three methods of connecting the right hand to the left on the handle of the club. They are: interlocking, overlapping and 10-finger. Interlocking and overlapping are the most common. Whichever way you like to connect the right hand is OK. It is not an overwhelmingly important issue, although I would advise beginners, all women and older men to use the 10-finger grip. I feel this makes the right hand stronger and the up-cocking action easier.

To *interlock,* the little finger of the right hand and the index finger of the left hand intertwine—they wrap around each other.

To *overlap,* the little finger of the right hand is placed along the crevice formed by the index and middle fingers of the left hand. Most golfers find this more comfortable than the in-

terlocking grip. My own grip is a modification of the overlap. I set the little finger of the right hand on top of the left-hand index finger. I do this because I have short fingers.

With the *10-finger* grip, there is no interlocking or overlapping. All the fingers of both hands are on the handle of the club.

Whichever connection you use, the right thumb always angles to the left across the top of the handle, and the hand *completely covers the left thumb.*

Some golfers turn the right hand to the right so the palm is under the handle and the left thumb is exposed. They usually hook or slice their shots badly. Other golfers turn the right hand far to the left, or "on top" of the handle. The left thumb is covered, but the position is too extreme and promotes a sliced ball.

You know your clubs are correct size when tips of fingers on left hand just touch pad of hand. No part of hand overlaps butt-end of club handle.

If the left thumb is on top of the grip, as I recommend, and it can't be seen, you will have a very functional, sound right-hand grip. Another measure of whether the right hand is in a correct position is its palm. The angle of the right palm should match the angle of the lead edge of the clubface; the palm faces the target exactly the same as the clubface does.

When the two hands are together in a complete grip, and you look down at them from the address position, you will see a V formed by the thumb and index finger of the right hand. That V should point at the center of your body.

(See illustrations for all the above.)

Grip pressure

How much pressure should be exerted on the handle? How hard, or soft, should you hold the club? Some instruction says to hold the club like a feather—light and gentle—so there is no tension built up in the muscles. Other instruction says to hold the club as tightly as you can, because you're making a forceful and precise swing action and don't want the club coming loose in your hands.

The reasoning in both cases is good, but I think the two are extreme.

Grip pressure is a very individualistic thing, a personal feeling that cannot be scientifically prescribed. What is vise-like to one person may be a bit loose for someone else. For myself, I like to have a good hold of the club because, as noted earlier, the clubhead weighs about 100 pounds when swung for a full shot.

As a general rule regarding grip pressure, you want firmness without losing flexibility and freedom of motion.

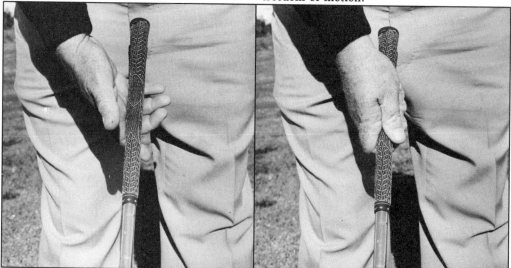

Club is held more in the fingers of the right hand, for greater club control. With right hand in final position, the thumb angles across the handle. The V points to the center of your body.

When the grip is completed, the angle of the right palm matches the angle of the lead edge of the clubface; both face the target. The left thumb is completely covered.

Keep pressure constant

The amount of grip pressure can't be taught in a specific way. But I can say that the amount of pressure should be commensurate with the degree of force the shot requires. In other words, when hitting a driver off the tee of a 450-yard hole, or a 6-iron out of thick, tangled grass, grip pressure should be firm. The pressure is lighter when playing short pitches, very firm for chip shots.

But most important of all, *MAINTAIN THE SAME GRIP PRESSURE FROM THE BEGINNING TO THE END OF THE SWING FOR ALL SHOTS.* Too many golfers hold the club very tightly at address, often because of mental anxiety, and when more pressure develops from the force of the swing, the hands simply cannot take the stress and come loose. Then, during the downswing, the hands will instinctively firm up or regrip the club. Old pros called this "playing the piccolo." However it's termed, when grip pressure changes during a swing the angle of the clubface is likely to change, too. That is not the way to play consistent golf.

KEEP GRIP PRESSURE CONSTANT, whatever that pressure may be.

'Weak' and 'strong' grips—a brief, one-sided debate

The grip with the left hand that I ask my students to take is what other golf teachers call the "weak" position. That's because it helps prevent the hand from turning over on the downswing. Most golf teachers, and golfers, feel the left hand must turn over in order to hit a stronger shot. Thus, my left-hand position is "weak."

The opposite, of course, is to turn the left

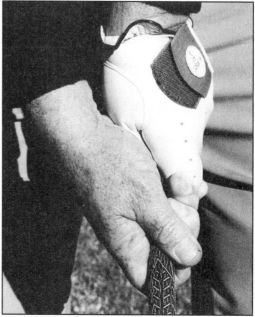

(Left) Traditional 'strong' grip, left hand twisted to golfer's right.

hand to the right into a "strong" position. Now the hand can more readily turn over.

For the left hand, I reverse that designation. My left-hand position is "strong," not "weak," because with it you have absolute control of the club. Therefore, there is going to be almost no change in the angle of the clubface. It makes *you* the master of the club. *Control is strength!*

Let me put it another way. The left-hand position I teach is exactly the position the hand should be in at impact with the ball. Ideally, it forms a 90-degree angle with the target line. The closer you set the hand to that position at address, the easier it is to get the correct position at impact.

As for the right-hand position, when the hand

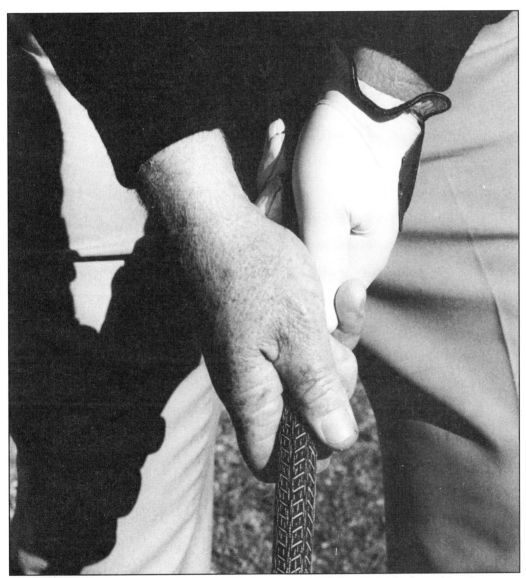

Traditional 'weak' grip, back of left hand facing target at 90-degree angle. I consider the 'weak' grip strong, because it's in same position it should be at impact.

is turned to the right, or under the handle, traditionalists call this the "strong" position. So do I, but I don't recommend the position because it creates an imbalance. Set the right hand on the handle as I've described it, and it will be *in balance* with the left hand. The total grip will be neither weak nor strong. It will be neutral.

You will hear a lot about weak and strong grip positions when you examine various other instructional ideas. But I don't make much of a fuss over the grip in my teaching. The grip should be simple in its form and in its formulation. The neutral or balanced grip satisfies both those needs.

I do, however, put a lot of emphasis on the address.

The Address

Move into address position begins from behind ball, to get overall perspective of shot to be played.

A key to playing good golf is a good address —standing correctly at the ball. If you do, you increase your chances of taking the club away from the ball correctly and making an effective downswing and through-swing. Most often, the better the address, the better the player.

The alignment of the body and club at the ball is very often the main cause of swing problems. The first thing a golfer should do when his game goes off is check out his address positions. That's where most of the tour pros go first, and often that's as far as they have to go.

When you are hitting the ball well, make a permanent note of every detail of your address position so you have a reference guide to call on when you are hitting the ball poorly. Note your ball-to-feet alignment, weight distribution, width of stance and all the other elements that will be described on the following pages.

Getting to the ball

You begin every golf shot before you get into the actual address position. The preliminary is essential to a good address. Start every golf shot from about three to five yards behind the ball, facing the target. This gives you an overall perspective of your target and its relation to everything around it—hazards, mounds, pin position on the green and so on. This is when you pick out the line you want the ball to take and where you want it to land. You make a mental picture of the ball's planned trajectory. It is also when you visualize the parallel line where you place your feet. Finally, it's when

At ball clubface is square to target, and feet are on a line about two feet left of it, depending on height of player and club used.

you take your grip on the club. When you move to the ball, come to it directly from the side—at a right angle to the ball and parallel to the target. A lot of golfers, including pros, come to the ball on an oblique angle (see illustration). This can lead to poor alignment, as it is disorienting in relation to the target. Better to walk into address position with your body square, just as it's to be when the swing starts.

Place clubhead first

With your feet side by side and very close together, place the clubhead behind the ball with the face at a 90-degree angle to the target line. As a guide for obtaining this angle, use a combination of the shaft and the grooves on the clubface—the two must be in alignment with each other.

I see too many golfers set their feet first at address, then the clubface. Nine times out of 10 they end up aiming at the wrong place. Set the clubface and shaft in position first, and at the correct angle to the target line, and you have a guide for getting the body square.

There's nothing worse than seeing a solidly hit shot go off line because of poor alignment at address.

AIM THE CLUBFACE AND SHAFT FIRST, THEN FIT YOUR BODY TO THEM.

Width of stance

Next, spread your feet. How far apart? The general rule: the distance between the *insides of the feet is equal to the width of the shoulders*. I go along with that, but tend to favor a slightly narrower spread so the player is forced to maintain good balance. Also, the narrower the space between your feet, the more flexibility you have

for making the lower-body turn.

Some people advocate a wider spread of the feet for stability and a feeling of strength. But a wide stance causes a lack of lower-body mobility. It creates a tension, a freezing sensation, that promotes lateral upper-body movement. I don't think a relatively narrow stance will necessarily cause a loss of balance, but I *know* excessive upper-body movement to the sides produces poor shots.

THE STANCE SHOULD BE WIDE ENOUGH FOR STABILITY, BUT NEVER SO WIDE THAT YOU LOSE MOBILITY. I prefer flexibility.

Ball-to-feet alignment

The alignment of the ball in relation to the feet is a very important factor in the address. Today's golfers are hitting the ball much farther generally, not so much because of modern equipment, but because they are playing the ball more forward in their stance; it is more off the left foot.

Players of past generations tended to align the ball more toward the right foot, especially with irons. Maybe it was because of the kind of grass they played from, although I think it had more to do with their wanting to avoid hooking the ball. In any case, they were in a sense hitting the ball from behind them. A good analogy to this is in tennis or baseball. Nobody drills a solid forehand crosscourt or pounds out a home run when the ball is almost past his body. The most powerful stroke with a bat, racquet or golf club comes when the *arms are extending forward into the ball* at impact.

In terms of my swing concept then, the more the ball is set forward in the stance, the better you make the underhand-toss motion. The

Position clubface first, at correct angle to target, then set feet and body in relation to clubface to get proper alignment to target. Feet close together at start helps visualize correct ball-to-foot relationship when feet are spread.

Width of stance is relatively narrow, and ball is played about two inches inside left heel for most clubs.

hands will definitely be fully uncocked, and the arms and club fully extended at impact. You will have that sense of getting the clubhead *under the ball* with the irons and fairway woods.

What do I mean by forward? For standard full iron shots, play the ball *no more than two inches inside the left heel,* and *for every iron in the bag.* With the fairway woods, play the ball off the left heel; and with the driver, between the heel and arch of the foot (see illustration).

I am striving to produce a natural motion. That's why I teach the pendulum-type swing. A pendulum, *no matter its length,* always come back to the bottom of its arc in the same place. So will a golf club, no matter the length of its shaft.

With a real pendulum and a golf swing, you can determine where the bottom of the swing arc will be. For the pendulum you adjust the

fulcrum. In golf, at address you arrange the alignment of the ball in relation to your feet. With the golf ball in the same approximate location every time, you can hit the ball more consistently solid and with the greatest possible clubhead speed.

Finding the relationship

The reason I recommend stepping into the address position with your feet close together is that you can better visualize the ball-to-foot relationship once the feet are spread. But even then, because width of stance varies according to the individual, I advise two other guides.

For all golfers, no matter their size or width of stance, the ball should be aligned in the same relationship to the head and left shoulder. To be precise, have the ball on a line with the left side of your face. *AT NO TIME IS THE*

HEAD IN FRONT OF THE BALL!

Or, the center of your chest is always *completely behind the ball.*

On the balls of your feet, with minimal knee flex

In general, I want the body-weight distribution at address to favor the left side. *Body weight is never less on the left than on the right* (except on an uphill lie). For standard iron shots it is a 60-40 ratio, but on chips and pitches it can be as much as 70-30. For wood shots, the ratio is 55-45.

Otherwise, overall weight is *concentrated on the balls of the feet.* You don't want your weight back on your heels, because you are essentially flat-footed and lose mobility and flexibility. You want to feel light on your feet, so you can use them in the swing. When you're on the balls of your feet you can use the "quick" muscles—the front muscles—of your legs.

At address, you should be able to raise and lower your heels. At first you may feel you're leaning too far forward, but that's probably because you've been on the back of your heels all the time. The body seeks stability and balance. When the weight is on the balls of the feet, you will instinctively move toward the right heel on the backswing and toward the left heel on the downswing. Thus, by starting the swing on the balls of the feet, you not only produce stability and flexibility, but promote the proper rotation of the body around its axis. Your body should always turn away from, not toward, the ball.

This lightness of body is further enhanced by keeping the legs almost straight at address. *You want to be as tall as you can from the WAIST*

Overall weight is concentrated on balls of feet, and there is very little flex in knees (left). Both encourage maximum flexibility in swing, and "standing-tall" posture from waist down. Weight on heels and knees flexed (right), inhibit mobility and rotation.

DOWN. There should be only the slightest amount of flex—just enough so you are not locked in. I definitely do not like to see a "sitting-down" position. This, too, inhibits mobility. And rotation is limited because of the tension that deep-flexing creates.

Don't Squat! Stand Tall! Minimum knee-flex allows you to stand taller at the ball during the downswing.

Distance from the ball

Everyone's arms should hang the same way at address. That is, *almost perfectly vertical.* You always want your hands as low as possible, and they are lowest when hanging straight down. They do not project outward as though reaching for the ball, nor are they held very close in to the body, both of which produce tension. Tense muscles are shortened muscles. That tension is reflected in the swing, which is too short and quick. Let the arms hang naturally, neither too stiff nor relaxed, so they can swing freely.

When the arms hang vertically, with the spine as straight as possible and bending at the waist, the distance you stand from the ball is determined.

There is a guide for checking that your arms are hanging correctly and that you are the proper distance from the ball in relation to the club you're using. *The butt of the club will be approximately a hand-width, or from four to six inches, from your body* (see illustration). If it is less than four inches, you will be crowding the ball; if it is more, you will be stretching.

Hands low, club on heel

I want the hands to hang as low as possible, while maintaining the correct posture. You can do this without slumping your shoulders or flexing your knees, by *pushing the heels of the hands slightly downward.* This will be a kind of preview of the up-cocking movement at the start of the swing. It will also create the slight kinking where the wrists join the hands that I spoke of earlier.

In pushing the hands down this way, the clubhead will be tilted back so *the toe is raised off the ground.* The club will be sitting on the back third of the flange. I think everyone should play golf with the club set this way at address. I say this because in the downswing the shaft bows downward. The down-bowing brings the sole of the club flush to the ground at impact.

Posture

Your overall posture at the address will feature:

—Upper legs straight, lower legs very slightly flexed. Upper body and legs leaning slightly forward toward the ball.

—Back straight, a small bend at the waist.

—Head high.

You are, in a sense, standing up from the waist down. It's what I call the Southern California Posture—chest out, shoulders back, butt back—as opposed to the Finishing School Posture—chest in, shoulders slumped.

Aiming with your body

At address, you set up to aim your clubface and your body. But they do not aim at the same thing.

When the clubhead is put behind the ball, it is on the target line and the clubface is aimed at the target. Your feet are spread along the parallel line, and by keeping your knees, hips and shoulders square, your entire body runs

Correct distance from the ball is obtained when the butt of club is about a hand-width from your body.

along that parallel line. Thus, your body is aimed to the left of the target. The distance it is aimed left of the target is the distance between your feet and the ball and clubhead.

This is as it should be. However, many golfers tend not to do this. They are inclined to aim their feet, and thus the whole body, at the target itself. If they do this, and maintain a correct alignment of the hands and club at address, the clubface will be aimed to the right of the target. You cannot aim both the clubface, and your body, at the target without distorting the clubhead and/or the angle of your wrists and hands at address. The clubface will have to be closed *in relation to your body,* or your hands will have to be behind the ball. Some golfers who get into this error at address will try to adjust by turning only their hips and shoulders to the left, while keeping their feet aimed at the target. This is another distortion, one that breeds tension and restricts the length and smooth flow of the backswing.

Your body aimed to the left of the target promotes a balanced, coordinated, natural swing plane.

To make a proper turn of the left side on the downswing and through-swing, I want the left foot opened—angled about 30 to 40 degrees so the foot is pointing *out toward the target area.*

If the left foot is square, there will be some resistance to the turning of the left hip in the downswing and through-swing. You may have to force the turn, and that will throw you out of balance.

With the left foot open, you have better balance and less strain on the left ankle, knee and hip.

The right foot can be square to the parallel line. Actually, I don't mind seeing it opened

about 10 degrees to the right to facilitate an easier backswing turn.

However, *you never want the right foot turned in and pointing toward the target.* This restricts the backswing turn, and forces the right ankle to roll outside the foot.

Waggle to get loose

Just about everybody who plays golf, even the rank beginner trying it for the first time, will swing the club back and forth or up and down before starting the swing. It's a natural, instinctive thing to do. It is a release of tension, a loosening up. It's the same thing as a baseball hitter swinging his bat back and forth a few times while waiting for the pitch. In golf this is called a "waggle."

Some golfers are what I call "dead-stickers"; they don't waggle at all. You can play this way, but all the fine players have some motion before starting the swing itself. It's like the conductor of an orchestra, who has a prebeat movement. He swings his arms into the 'one,' so everyone starts together on 'three.' The waggle establishes a rhythm and coordination.

Everyone finds his own waggle; there is not one that is necessarily better than another. Some golfers cock their heads to one side, some raise and lower their feet in place, others squeeze and unsqueeze the handle of the club a few times. I like to rock my body slightly from the inside of the right toe to the left.

The waggle is a matter of choice, but I will offer one suggestion. For pitch shots, using my swing concept, you might waggle the club in a circular motion. This promotes flexibility in the wrists and a soft feel.

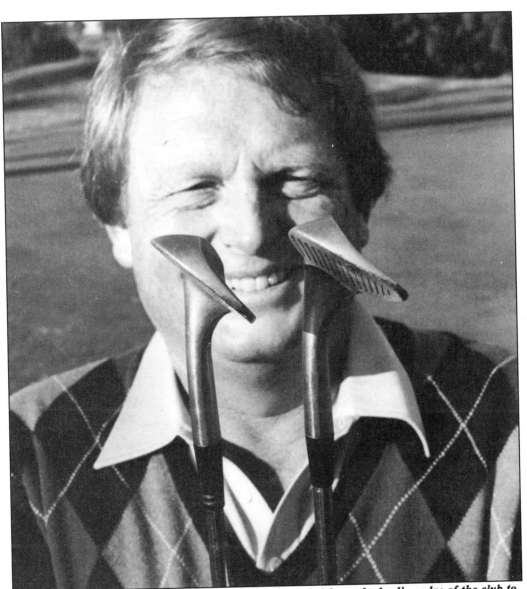

The sand wedge on my left has "bounce," the sole angled from the leading edge of the club to the back of its flange.

ging action, which is why the incline is called "bounce." The clubhead goes under the ball, but never touches it. The ball is exploded out of the bunker by the force of the flying sand.

The same principle applies to my pitch shot, even though the ball is actually hit by the clubhead. For the high and medium-high pitches, the clubhead hits the grass behind the ball and moves parallel to the ground to impact and slightly beyond. Contact is made low enough below the center of the ball so that the built-in loft of the club raises it up into the air. But the swing path of the club at impact has more to do with the height of the shot than the loft of the club. The underhand-toss motion and the club rising quickly when the hands recock after impact create much of the elevation.

Because the ball is hit with the clubhead moving parallel to the ground, it has no significant spin on it. There is some spin, but never enough to affect flight or landing characteristics. As I've said, on a flat surface the ball generally takes a short bounce and rolls only a few feet forward after landing. That short bounce indicates you've hit the shot correctly. A shot with excessive spin will take a much longer, skipping-type bounce.

The shot provides a much greater margin for error than when trying to hit the ball first. For my standard pitch shot you hit about two inches behind the ball. But if you hit as much as five behind it when playing out of fairly long grass, you'll still get an adequate result. If you err on the other side and hit a little closer to the ball, say only an inch behind it, you will still get a usable shot; you'll get the same distance in the air but probably a lower trajectory and a bit more roll after landing.

The face of the sand wedge laid open (left), in closed position (right), and square (far right).

Pitch shots should be played with the face square to the target line for greater consistency in height and distance.

For pitch-shot the stance is slightly open, weight is on balls of feet, there is no slump in the shoulders.

In a word, you can't really miss the shot, as that term is conventionally used. You'll almost always get the ball out of trouble and somewhere near your objective. This is very important, since the shot is often used from in close to a green that you didn't reach in the regulation number of strokes. You are trying to save a par but to do no worse than make a bogey. You definitely do not want to make a double bogey.

There are three priorities for this shot. In order of importance they are: (1) Get out of trouble, (2) get on the green, (3) get close to the hole. Many double bogeys result from trying to hit too perfect a pitch shot and coming up short, usually hitting the ball into a bunker or long grass. I want to take as much risk out of the game as possible. With my pitch shot, the ball will always go farther because the flange hitting the ground behind it creates clubhead speed. You are less often short of your distance—if anything, you'll be a bit longer.

Addressing the pitch shot

Do not lay the clubface open at address so it is aimed to the right of the target. You are not playing the traditional "cut-shot" in which an open clubface is compensated for by swinging across the ball from outside to in.

FOR MY PITCH SHOT YOU MAKE THE BASIC INSIDE-TO-OUT SWING, with the clubface square at address.

I don't recommend the cut-shot, because it's not consistent for distance. When the clubface is open the ball tends to roll across it and come off with sidespin. Thus, height and distance vary. When the clubface is square at impact, the ball sort of freezes on the face—stays on it longer.

Club is drawn slightly more inside just before downswing begins to make up for minimal body turn for pitch shot.

Clubhead rises quickly at the start of backswing, and begins to move inside, in relation to body. There is just a slight turn of the right side at completion of backswing, and wrists are fully cocked. Body height remains same throughout.

At impact hands and wrists are fully released. There is a very definite turn of the body to the left as the club is swung under the ball and up. The clubhead very quickly gets above the butt-end of the club.

From facing angle, you see better other elements of the pitch-shot technique. Stance is narrow at heels, hands are on line with the ball, body weight is distributed on both legs. Up-cocking of wrists and turn of shoulders initiates backswing.

Hands have begun to uncock early in downswing to promote the underhand-toss action. The left leg straightens and left hip turns away from ball to promote inside-to-out swing path. Left hand and arm relax through impact area.

With a minimal turn of the right hip, and no significant shift of the weight to the right side, the up-cocking of the wrists and turn of shoulders create a very compact backswing, the body remaining at same height as at address.

You want the sense of the club moving under the ball and hitting up on it as though you were hitting it over a wall five yards in front of you. Even on this short shot, the right foot is raised, indicating proper movement. You don't play the pitch shot flat-footed.

Use your STANDARD GRIP. Grip pressure is important for the pitch shot, especially with the left hand. It wants to be relaxed for a good release through impact.

PLAY THE BALL OFF THE LEFT IN-STEP. This is a little more forward than for standard irons shots, but you want to *hit underneath,* not down on, the ball and with an underhand-toss motion. This alignment promotes both.

A narrow, open stance

The feet are only three to four inches apart *at the heels* to insure that you have some foot movement for this relatively light swing; this is not a power shot.

The stance is open. The left foot is slightly behind the parallel line, the toes angling out toward the target about 45 degrees. The right foot is square to, and on, the parallel line. (See illustration.) With this positioning of the left foot you will be more or less facing the target.

Stand on the balls of your feet, and be sure you're "standing tall" so you can make a full extension of your arms and the club at address.

To repeat, once you establish your distance from the ball and your posture at address, keep those measurements throughout the swing; your body should not drop or rise up at any time.

Hands never ahead

To prevent any possibility of the club digging into the ground, the hands are never forward of the ball at address. Keep them aligned even with the ball.

Hold the clubhead over the spot where you want it to make contact. If you're going to start

your flat spot two inches behind the ball, set the clubhead at that point, *but don't touch it.* As Paul Runyan puts it, you should "micro-scopically underreach"—the clubhead just bare-ly above the ground at address. It helps you keep your posture and your arms extended.

The pitch-shot swing

The backswing for the pitch shot begins just as it does for the standard shots. The hands are cocking up, creating a lever effect, as the shoulders begin to turn. However, because this is not a power-oriented shot and the stance is a little open, the right side tends not to turn as much in the backswing. You will swing the club inside to out in relation to your body, but

For highest trajectory, left side of face is four inches behind ball.

parallel to target line. Underhand motion causes clubhead to make a slight circle to the inside, which gives the appearance of a figure 8.

While the straightening of the left leg and the turning of the left hip will create an inside-to-out swing path; just as for the fuller shots, for the pitch the circling of the club to the inside increases this path angle. Visualize and feel the underhand-toss motion, and all the swing parts will fall in place.

You want to get the sense of the clubhead moving under the ball and hitting up on it. You're trying to raise the ball over that wall five yards in front of you. You get this feeling by *relaxing the left arm and hand through the impact area.*

The right hand and arm, and the club want to swing out toward the target. You never want the club to swing across the target line, but along it.

Adjustments for trajectory

When you want a certain trajectory for the pitch shot, the adjustment is made with your head and eyes, *not* the alignment of the ball in relation to your feet. The ball is always played off the left instep!

For the highest trajectory, the flat spot begins three to four inches behind the ball, so the club is starting to rise right after impact. *The left side of your face is four inches behind the ball.*

For medium trajectory, the flat spot begins two

For medium trajectory, left side of face is two inches behind ball.

For lowest trajectory, left side of face is over ball.

inches behind the ball, so the club is still parallel to the ground at impact. *The left side of your face is two inches behind the ball.*

For the lowest trajectory, the flat spot begins at the very end of the club's descent, or at the back of the ball. *The left side of your face is over the ball.*

In effect, you are setting your head *and body* in relation to the ball. Your weight distribution is automatically changed. It will be slightly more to the left when the left side of your face is over the ball than when it is four inches behind it. For the highest shot, your body is leaning slightly to the right relative to the position for the lowest shot.

Keep your eyes on the spot where you want the club to hit!

Finding the range

Do not back off the pitch shot. Many golfers, after they get the sense of the swing, have trouble gauging how hard to hit the ball for the distance. Most will not swing hard enough or make a big enough swing. Remember, most of the trouble is between you and the hole. It is much better to hit the ball a little too far than not far enough!

There are two schools of thought on how much swing to make for the distance. One is, you make a full-size swing for a full shot, a half-size swing for a half-shot, and so on down the line.

The other school of thought is mine. It begins with the premise that the hardest shot to hit is when the swing is *less than three-quarter length.* I want to eliminate swinging under three-quarters! I want the swing to be as large as possible and to vary its *speed.*

First you find out how far you hit the pitch shot with a full-size swing. Then you try to keep that same swing-size and change the speed to suit the distance needed. The slower swing will produce the softer, shorter shot. The firmer, more aggressive swing will make the ball go faster and farther.

The Three-wedge System

My concept of never making less than a three-quarter swing for any pitch shot ties into the Three-wedge System that I helped introduce a few years ago. That is, you carry *two* sand

A drill for getting a feel for pitch-shot distance and the under-hand toss motion is to actually toss balls underhanded to a green.

wedges and the pitching wedge. Each has a different loft. The 2-iron is left out of the set. (Remember, you're allowed to play with only 14 clubs.)

There is a 4-degree difference in loft between each club in the entire set. Thus, every club hits the ball a certain distance, or at least a different distance—the 2-iron goes about 15 yards farther than the 3-iron, the 3-iron about 15 yards farther than the 4-iron, and so on. In effect, there is a club for every 15 yards of approach-shot...until you get to around 75

yards from the green and closer. Then there are only two clubs available to cover the area. With three wedges in the bag, you have more versatility without having to vary your swing length.

The pitching wedge has 52 degrees of loft and can hit the ball at least 100 yards on average, maybe a little more. The middle sand wedge has 56 degrees of loft and can hit the ball 75 yards with a full swing, 40 to 45 yards with a three-quarter swing. The full sand wedge has 60 degrees of loft and can hit the ball around 60

Stand sideways to target as when hitting with a club, and toss balls underhanded. Start with a 5-yard "shot" and gradually increase distance in five-yard increments until you are tossing ball from 40 yards out.

yards with a full swing and 35 to 40 yards with a three-quarter swing.

The innovative part of the Three-wedge System is the inclusion of the 60-degree-loft sand wedge. It allows you to make a three-quarter swing to hit a ball only 40 yards and sometimes even less. You don't have to let up on your swing as much from in close to the green. You can swing relatively full and still get a soft shot.

A number of touring pros have adopted the Three-wedge System, but it is especially useful for the average golfer because he misses more greens with his approaches. A lot of those missed greens leave him with pitch shots within the 75-yard range. With three wedges he has one more club to help him in the scoring area of the course.

Why leave the 2-iron out of the bag? One look at any golfer's 2-iron and wedge will provide the answer. The 2-iron is shiny from little use, the wedge is dark with wear. As I said in my introduction, the last two shots on every hole are the most important. The first of those two shots is very often a short pitch shot, and the more clubs you have available for the scoring area, the better your scores will be.

A distance drill

But even if you carry three wedges, you still want to develop a feel for hitting the ball the right distance. To that end I use a couple of drills with my students.

In one of the drills, I have students actually toss balls underhanded. They take the regular address position and swing only the ball-tossing arm. They start by tossing balls five yards, then the distance is increased in five-yard increments up to around 40 yards. There is an excellent carryover when they begin hitting the shot with the sand wedge. The drill is also good for getting the sense of the underhand-toss motion.

In the second drill, they hit real pitch shots to four or five distances. First they hit 30-yard pitches and decrease the distance by five yards or so, and get it down to around five yards. You strike the ball with the club, but visualize tossing it underhand.

Chipping

With the pitch shot, your primary goal is to get the ball on the green within two-putt range of the hole. The occasional one-putt is a bonus. *The goal of the chip shot is to get the ball very close to the hole for a one-putt.* Holing out is the bonus.

A chip shot is a scoring shot. But many golfers make it a trouble shot by avoiding it. Some choose to putt a ball from the fringe of the green rather than chip it. Others try a pitch shot. Either way is not as positive an approach to golf as you should take. It is saying you cannot hit the ball properly with one of the shortest and simplest of strokes. To chip is to play golf the smartest way and make a good score. Chipping leaves less room for error.

Distance is the key factor in successful chipping, and when you putt from a few feet or more off a green you add a highly unreliable dimension to the shot. You must judge the speed of two or more different surfaces, and calculate how hard to hit the ball to get it through longer, rougher fringe grass without it going too fast for the much smoother and faster green. No one is good enough to make that calculation correctly all the time. It's hard to practice the shot—I've seldom seen anyone who does—and as Ben Hogan once said, "Never hit a shot on the golf course that you haven't practiced."

Golfers who use a high-lofted club from the fringes—a pitching wedge or 9-iron—and try to carry the ball most of the way to the hole and make it stop quickly, are trying a very low-percentage shot. The stroke must be very precise and must produce just the right amount of backspin to coordinate with how far the ball carries and then rolls. Some people can play this shot from the fringe. Bobby Locke always used a pitching wedge. He knew how the ball would react every time under all conditions. But, on the whole, it is not the most reliable way to play because the ball must be hit in the air too much.

The chipping system

With the chip shot you *always land the ball on the green.* The green is the smoothest surface you play on. You know you'll get the truest possible bounce and roll. You should never pitch or putt when you can chip, *and you can chip from much farther out than you think.* It's not a shot played only from a few feet off the green. A chip can be played from as much as 15 yards off the green; it depends on how much distance there is between the start of the green and the hole.

Chipping by the numbers

The idea in chipping is to get the ball on the ground and rolling as soon as possible. For chips shots when the ball is just a few feet off the green, the ball should land no less than one foot and no more than five feet into the green. This is the comfort zone that gives you a margin of safety against landing the ball in the fringe with a slightly mis-hit shot.

As a practice drill, I put a coin at the spot on the green where I want the ball to land and work on hitting balls in the air to that spot (see illustration).

With the basic criteria of where to land the ball established, the rest of the chipping system is even more a matter of numbers. There's a basic format that takes into account how much roll you get with each club used for chipping. Here's the format for the five different clubs to chip with—the pitching wedge, the 9-, 8-, 7- and 6-iron. There's a difference in how much roll is gotten with each club.

Pitching wedge—1 part in the air, 2 parts on the ground.

9-iron—1 part in the air, 3 parts on the ground.

The ball should have the same amount of roll no matter the loft of the ball or how far it is carried, because the stroke used produces the same kind of spin—lack of spin, actually—and from any sort of lie.

8-iron—1 part in the air, 4 parts on the ground.
7-iron—1 part in the air, 5 parts on the ground.
6-iron—1 part in the air, 6 parts on the ground.

That's the Flight-to-Roll Ratio. If you use this system there is no room for doubt about which club to use for each chip.

For example, you step off the total distance to the hole. Say you're 36 feet from the cup and have six feet of fringe to carry over. To be within the landing-area comfort zone, you will hit the ball about nine feet in the air. You divide the 9 into 36, and get 4. This is 1 part in the air, 3 parts on the ground. You use a 9-iron.

If you're 50 feet from the hole and seven feet off the green, you carry the ball 10 feet and run it 40 feet. One part in the air, 4 parts on the ground. You use an 8-iron.

It goes into the computer just like that. There should be no confusion about club selection, which is the cause for as many missed shots as any other thing in golf. That includes all areas of the game. Because so much of golf is mental, when you can make a decision and be comfortable with it, you will play better. Having control of distance is a very important key to successful golf.

You can see from the numbering system how the outer limit of a chip shot is determined and

Landing point on green—the light coin— is same from every distance back from the fringe. But club used from each distance is different, because of how far ball must carry to coin. Shot being played is with a 9-iron.

Chipping address and stroke: Ball is played off right foot. Hands are well ahead of ball, left hand even with left thigh.

when you must go to pitching. For instance, if you have 50 feet to the hole, and the hole is cut only 20 feet into the green, you must carry the ball 33 feet. That leaves only 17 feet to roll the ball, which is under the lowest flight-to-roll ratio of 1 part to 2. There is not enough rolling room, and since you don't want to land the ball in the fringe where the bounce will be uncertain, you pitch the ball.

I don't mean to make it sound absolutely cut-and-dry. If a green is slower than usual because the grass hasn't been cut, or it's wet from rain, or you're playing uphill or downhill, adjustments must be made within the system *in respect to how much the ball will roll.* Before every round and especially on a course where you're not familiar with the greens, don't only practice putts. Take some chipping practice, too, to see how the ball rolls. Hit some with a pitching wedge and with a 6-iron so both ends of the club-selection spectrum are covered.

It is important to have a basic system or program to work from. The less doubt you have, the better you play. Systems reduce doubt.

The chipping method

The number system for chipping is fairly constant not only because numbers don't change but because *the method of hitting the ball is the same for every club.*

The *pace* of stroke does not vary from club to club, or from one kind of lie to another.

A stroke for all reasons

Because I believe it is always better to chip than pitch, my chipping method is designed mainly to deal with the worst kinds of lies, when balls are down into rough, sometimes tangled grass—in a hole, so to speak. I want to get the ball out of that lie as cleanly as I can. To do so it takes a sharply descending stroke; that's the only way to get the job done. Chipping is

Elbows are pointed outward. Weight is distributed 70 percent on the left side. Stroke is very vertical with no wrist action or flat spot, and virtually no follow-through.

the only part of the game where I use this type of stroke—there is no flat spot in chipping. It works just as well for the better lies. There is no real difference in how the ball reacts. Thus, in order to build consistency into the game, I use the same chipping technique throughout—the same descending blow.

All the positions and mechanics I teach for chipping are different from the rest of my swing concepts. They are all designed to hit the ball very low, so the bounce will be as predictable as possible and the ball gets rolling almost immediately. The more consistent the ball flight, the more consistent the rolling distance.

The chipping grip and address

I prefer the 10-finger grip for chipping, just as I do for putting. I think it provides more control of the club. I would like you to give it a try. I believe you'll find it makes a real contribution to the execution of a good stroke.

However, the positioning of the hands that I teach is otherwise radically different and intrinsic to my chipping system.

This is a one-gear or one-lever stroke that is made only with the arms and shoulders, so I am very much interested in eliminating all wrist action. The hand position I teach for chipping is with that in mind. It is extremely restrictive, and at first may feel uncomfortable. But after a while you'll find it "hurts real good."

It is what I call the fingernails-up grip. The left hand is turned far to the left, the right hand far to the right. Both, in effect, are underneath the handle (see illustration). The fingernails of both hands are facing straight up. The left thumb and right thumb angle across the top of the handle. You'll find it easier to adopt this positioning using the 10-finger grip.

Choke down all the way on the club. The right hand might even be partially on the steel part of the shaft. That's OK. It will enhance your feel

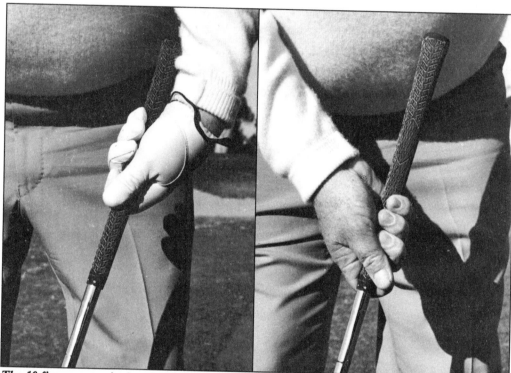

The 10-finger, no-wrist-break grip for chipping: Left hand turned far to the left so fingernails face up.

Right hand turned far to right so fingernails are up; the hand is set at very bottom of handle. You could even touch some of the shaft.

of the club.

Grip pressure is firm in both hands. This is a short and relatively abrupt stroke; you don't want any looseness.

Up close to the ball and facing the target

I catch a lot of golfers aiming the body to the right when chipping. This gives them a stilted perspective of the target that affects how they set the clubface. For this reason, I want the stance for chipping to be slightly open, the left foot pulled about three inches back from the parallel line (see illustration). You will be pretty much facing the target. This promotes a straight-back/straight-through stroke.

The feet are approximately one foot apart and *both are angled* toward the target—the left foot a little more so.

You're on the balls of your feet. There is only the slightest flex in the knees, just as for the other shots, and you should be leaning toward the target. The weight distribution is about 70-30 to the left. You're a kind of Leaning

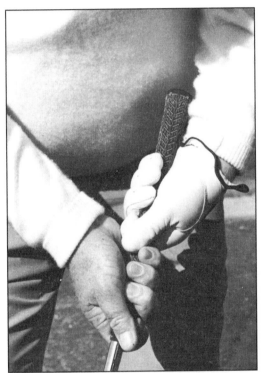

As a unit, hands are close together but do not actually connect— club is held in all 10 fingers. Grip pressure is firm in both hands.

Tower of Pisa, a position that makes a vertical stroke almost automatic.

You want to be standing fairly erect in terms of posture, with the shoulders level to each other.

The elbows are pointing outward so the arms form a cradle. This further prevents wrist action in the swing.

THE BALL IS PLAYED APPROX-IMATELY SIX INCHES DIRECTLY OFF THE TOES OF THE RIGHT FOOT. Your head is in front of the ball.

With the ball played so far back in the stance, the hands must be well ahead of it at address. In fact, the left hand should be just opposite the left thigh (see illustration).

The hands are held high—arched upward—so the club is a perfect extension of the left arm and just about vertical. The more upright you stand the club at address, the better.

To get the club this vertical, *the clubhead rests on its front half, on the toe, with the heel of the club well off the ground.* The clubface is aimed squarely at the hole.

Setting the clubhead this way may seem strange, but there is a very good reason for it. When the club hits the ground in the downstroke, the heel and its immediate extension, the shaft and hands, keep moving.

On the other hand, when the clubhead is set

For the chip, clubhead rests on its front half with heel off ground, a position that consistently produces clean, solid hits.

in the conventional manner with the sole completely flush with the ground, the heel can hit the ground first. If the grass is long, the heel can get snagged in it. In either instance, the flow of the swing is stopped and the clubface twists closed so the ball often doesn't get airborne; and it usually goes well left of the target.

None of this occurs when the clubhead is set at address with the heel well off the ground.

It might be that many golfers hit poor chip shots (then begin using a putter) because they are playing with the sole of the club flat on the ground at address and catching the heel in the ground. Furthermore, when the clubhead is flat at address, the tendency is to swing the club around instead of up and down. That plane can also cause the heel to snag and stop the shaft and hands from moving through.

Aiming the chip

I emphasize aiming the chip, just as I do all the other shots, but only before the stroke. Set up properly, with clubface square to the target line, then forget about it and think only of the stroke path and distance. *Concentrating too much on aim builds tension.*

Besides, I've never seen anyone able to read the break of a green correctly every time from the length that chip shots are usually played. No one can say for certain that a 30-foot chip shot will break 3⅞ inches, or whatever. You may be able to estimate a two-foot break, but there is no way anyone is going to be pinpoint precise about any break in a green. (The same goes for putting, as I will point out in the next chapter.) You can, **or should, be very specific about distance, though.**

The chipping stroke: up and down and down-the-line

You may have noticed before that I said *the shaft and hands* must move through the shot, and that I did not say the clubhead. That's an important distinction. The central idea when playing the chip shot is that you don't want to *hit the ball with the clubhead.* If you even think that way, you may move the clubhead forward but the shaft will almost always move backward at the same time. That is a hinging or flipping action that does not belong in the chip shot. It leads to hitting behind the ball and "dumping" it far short of the hole.

To prevent this kind of hinging, I like the butt of the club to be set against the left forearm, even digging in a little, *and never moving off the arm during the entire stroke.* The shaft is simply an extension of the forearm, and the two work as a single unit. At teaching sessions I tie the handle of the club to the left forearms of students so they can only swing the club with the arms, and get the sense of keeping the handle from going in one direction and the clubhead going in another (see illustration).

In other words, in the stroke for the chip shot the *clubhead and handle move in the same direction all the time.* The arc of the stroke is up and down, its path straight back and straight through along the target line. The clubhead never moves off the target line, and the clubhead remains square to it at all times.

To instill in students just how vertical I want the chip stroke to be, I ask them to make contact with *the ground* half an inch to one inch *in front of the ball.* The ball is hit just below its middle, with the club moving sharply downward (see illustration).

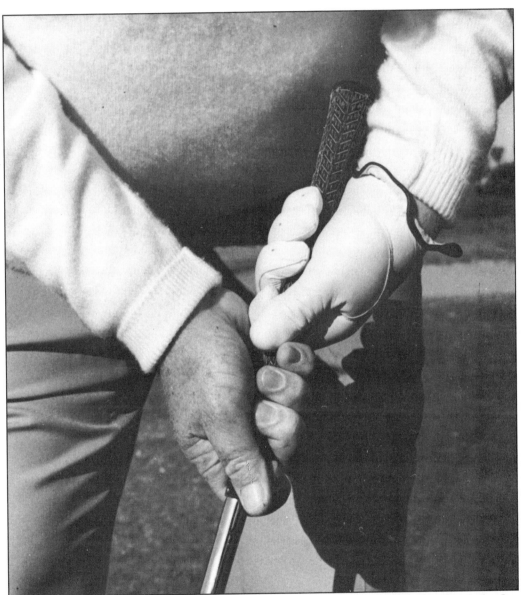

For the chip, handle of club rests along left forearm and never moves off during the stroke. In practice session, tie handle to arm to learn feel of clubhead and handle moving in same direction throughout stroke.

The ball may occasionally be hit a little "thin" with this stroke—the clubhead not getting all the way down to the ground—and the shot will not be as controlled. But that's the best way to miss. The ball seldom goes too far past the hole and thin shots have been known to stop right at the cup. However, when you hit behind the ball—catch it "fat" and dump it—it is very rarely going anywhere near the cup. As the saying goes, "Hit 'em thin to win."

Follow-through is minimal, at most

There is no real need to follow through, although you may get a short one when playing off a good lie. You just pop the club into the ground.

To think *no follow-through* is to help prevent any hitting with the right hand during the stroke. Put it this way: *The club never passes the left arm.* All the hit you need to achieve your flight-to-roll ratio derives from the length of the backstroke. The longer the backstroke, the harder you will hit the ball.

The basic chipping stroke is short and firm.

The pendulum pace of the stroke

As mentioned earlier, the swing path of the chipping stroke is straight back/straight through and the arc is up and down. Just like a pendulum and with the same tempo. The stroke is not faster or slower at any time. It is the same speed in both directions *and for all lengths of shot.*

YOU DON'T HIT AT THE BALL SO MUCH AS YOU SWING THROUGH IT.

Distance is controlled by the length of the stroke, not its speed.

With experience and practice, you'll know how much backswing you need for the distance of a shot. But it is always a good idea to take a few practice swings before hitting your chips during a round. Simulate the tempo and the exact length of stroke you feel you need, and carry that feeling into the shot itself.

Putting

Distance is everything

The most important thing about putting is control of distance. No one can one-putt every green, but there will always be a few one-putts and if you don't three-putt you get to keep them. Three-putting is almost always the result of poor distance, not direction. The first putt is either too long or too short. I've never seen a good putter who didn't have control of his speed and therefore his distance. There are putters who just reach the hole and "die" the ball in, and there are bolder putters who drill it in there. But the thing they both have in common is the ball always rolls at the same speed. Speed and distance are synonymous.

A consistent speed makes "reading" the line of putts more reliable. Let's say a putt has a break from right to left, and the ball is hit on the correct line but too hard. It will not break enough, or soon enough, and miss the hole on the "high side." If the same putt is hit too slowly, it will break too much and miss below and left of the hole. To make a breaking putt you need speed as much as direction. The golfer who time after time hits his putt at the same rate of speed feeds that consistency into his judgment of the contour of the green and makes a lot of putts. Good putters have the ball going into the hole at the same rate of speed every time, and *from any length*.

It is difficult to get across to people that everybody misses putts more often than they make them, and that some are made and some are missed *by accident*. A ball hit well may roll over a small defect in the green that can't be seen with the naked eye, and the ball is knocked off line...or on line. The longer the putt, the greater is the chance of this happening.

Then, of course, golfers may read the correct

line of a putt and hit the ball perfectly, but miss because they have not aimed the club correctly. A study of tour pros a few years ago showed that more than 75 percent of the 100 players tested aimed to the right to varying degrees. I think the percentage is even higher among average golfers. A lot of it has to do with the set-up. Too many golfers look at the ball from an angle either "inside" or "outside" it. They lean too far forward and their eyes are beyond, or outside, the ball; when they look along the target line, they see an elliptical curve from left to right. If their eyes are inside the ball they see the curve from right to left. They adjust the clubface to what they are seeing and end up aiming incorrectly.

That's why your eyes must look straight down on the ball. When you look straight down

T square formed by printing on ball and top edge of putter creates perfectly aimed setup.

you see only straight lines.

There's a method I teach for aiming the blade with a putter that has a mark, or line, on its top edge at the "sweet spot." Place the ball, with its name or other printing aimed down the line of putt. Then set the putter behind the ball so the mark on it and the writing on the ball are dead in line with each other. That will put the blade at a perfect 90-degree angle—"square"—to the target line (see illustration).

If the putter doesn't have a mark, the printing on the ball can alone guide you to a square blade at address. You get a T-square effect from the conjunction of the printing and the blade itself.

But even if you've aimed the putter perfectly, made a beautiful pendulum-paced stroke and the grass is as smooth as glass, if the putt is *13 feet long and longer and the ground is not perfectly*

level, it may not go in anyway because you didn't read the break correctly. Don't feel badly. When I was a kid Paul Runyan told me never to practice putts of more than 12 feet, because that's about the maximum distance you can have some positive thoughts about making them. A recent study proved that out. The odds on making a 13-foot putt and a 39-footer are identical. As I mentioned in the chapter on chipping, the best any golfer can hope for is a good *estimate* of how much a breaking putt will break.

Therefore, as I also mentioned in the chapter on chipping, you put a lot less pressure on yourself when you focus primarily on distance. People who have the putting "yips" are usually trying to guide their putts, because they are worried more about the line than the stroke. Guiding the putter creates tension, and from tension comes the nervous, jerky "yip" stroke.

Don't try to steer the ball, just go ahead and hit it with a smooth, natural stroke. Ideally, you'll knock the ball in, and the worst that can happen is the ball stops right beside the hole for an easy tap-in. Do everything you can to determine the line of a putt, set up to hit the ball on that line, then *concentrate ONLY on hitting the ball the correct distance.*

Developing the pace of the stroke

The key to hitting putts the correct distance is in the pace of the stroke. Watch a good putter practice 10-footers, and you'll see that he swings the putter back and through at the same speed every time. He is very conscious of how far he is hitting the ball, and every stroke is the same size. I will tell you what I mean by *same size* in a minute; it has to do with my number system for putting.

Then there are the players who are aiming all the time and not paying enough attention to distance. They tend to be inconsistent. The ball is hit too hard one time, and it goes too far. The next time, it is hit too softly, often because they are compensating for the putt hit too hard, and the putt comes up short. They are always guessing. It's important to know how hard to hit the ball.

There was another survey done on putting. Ten of the best putters in the game were tested, and it was found they had very little in common as far as stroke path. Some swung the putter inside to out, some a little inside to square, some straight back and through. But the one thing they all did was stroke the ball within *a thousandth of a second at 32 feet per second*, which is the force of gravity. They all swung the putter back and through at the same speed.

For every foot of putt, an inch of stroke

Most golfers don't increase or decrease the *sizes* of their strokes very much, they change the force or speed of them. They have their priorities backward. *The pace of the stroke is the same for all putts.* Distance is achieved by increasing or decreasing the *size* of the stroke. This is where my number system comes in.

I found that, in my case, if I swing the putter an inch back from the ball and an inch past it, the ball goes one foot. If I swing it six inches back and six inches through, the ball goes six feet. Therefore, I step off the footage from my ball to the hole to determine how long my stroke will be, and after setting up and aiming, make the stroke by the numbers. As long as *the size of the stroke is identical on both sides of the ball,* its pace shouldn't change.

If the greens are a little faster than usual, an adjustment is made. For a six-foot putt, let's say, stroke size may be for a five-footer. If the green is slower than usual, make the stroke seven inches back and seven inches through.

My system works up to around 25 feet. If you have a 30-footer or longer, you can't swing the putter that far in both directions. Now you must increase the *speed* of the stroke. *But that speed is also constant.* You don't take the putter back slowly and accelerate through or vice versa. It is still a pendulum stroke. There's a beat to it and the beat doesn't change. It's one-two, one-two. Not onnne-two, onnne-two, or one-twooo, one-twooo.

I have a drill for teaching this system. I use three tees and the ball I'm going to hit. I put my ball down, and right across from it stick a tee in the ground. Then I place one tee 10 inches behind, and another 10 inches ahead of the middle tee; all three are on the line of the putt. They are the guideline. The ball is stroked with the putter going 10 inches back and 20 inches through—to the back tee then to the forward tee. At first the pace may be different from what you're used to, but you will get the rhythm to the point where it is the same in both directions.

Not everyone will hit the ball exactly 10 feet with this setup because not everyone's touch is quite the same. *But the ball will be hit the same distance every time,* whatever that may be. No force need be applied! If you have the correct speed and the right direction, the ball will go in the hole just about every time. You can't always have the direction, but you can always have the speed, so it's a shame to waste the correct direction when you have it because your speed is incorrect.

At address, eyes are directly over ball. Stroke is straight back and through, and same distance in each direction. Tees are used in practice putting to develop consistency in the length of the stroke on both sides of the ball.

The drill also encourages an evenly paced stroke, which is the result of shoulders and arms moving club, not the hands. Never hit the ball on the upswing, but always at very bottom of downswing. A pendulum has maximum acceleration at the very bottom of swing, when the putter is accelerating. When ball is hit in upswing, the club is decelerating.

The ball should have no sidespin, only perfect overspin. Only in the follow-through will the putterhead rise up, and it should be allowed to, but in proportion to how far it rises in the backstroke.

Do everything you can to determine the line of the putt, set up to hit ball on that line, then concentrate only on hitting the ball the correct distance. Ball is played just inside left heel, with feet and body squared off.

Weight is on balls of feet and about 70 percent of the left side. Stance is a little wider than for the other shots, for stability.

The arms form a cradle, with elbows akimbo, to encourage an arms and shoulders stroke. The butt of the club, the hands, arms and shoulders all move as a single unit in the perfect pendulum stroke.

Swing the putter

I definitely *do not* advocate an all-wrist stroke. An orthopedic surgeon once told me that there are about four times as many nerves in your hands and wrists than in your shoulders and arms. Which is to say, if you're in a pressure-putt situation you don't want to—can't—depend on so vast and complicated a collection of sensitive physical parts. You're better off hitting the ball with your arms and shoulders. There should be no wrist motion. There are fine putters who have some, but the less the better.

The swing path

The optimum putt has no sidespin at all; the ball has perfect overspin. Nevertheless, there have been great putters who had sidespin on the ball. Some cut it with left-to-right spin. Dow Finsterwald and Bobby Locke hooked the ball, Locke with an extremely inside-to-out putting stroke. However, all those sidespin putters were great because they did it the *same way every time,* and every putt reacted the same way. The point, of course, is that you can putt well with any swing path as long as you are consistent with it.

However, the problem with those stroke paths is that they're often the result of a wristy action. The blade does not stay on the target line for the entire stroke. I feel that just makes it harder to consistently control distance and accuracy.

That's why I prefer a stroke path that is as much straight back and straight through as possible. It's a one-gear stroke that uses the shoulders and arms. The blade stays on the target line throughout the stroke, *and so does the butt of the club, the hands and the arms.* The shoulders, the arms and the *whole* club are a single unit. They are the pendulum—not the clubhead. The fulcrum is the neck, not the wrists.

Wristy putting may be OK for young kids who are nerveless, but they won't be young forever. What's more, arm-and-shoulder putters are less prone to cold streaks.

Contact—the club on the level

There's a school of putting that says you should hit up on the ball to make it roll. It will roll all right, but not the way it should. Hitting the ball just as the putter begins to rise makes the ball more or less dive into the grass. It "bites" into the grass and produces what I call a "heavy ball" that doesn't always run true.

Also, the tendency when hitting on the up-swing is to swing the putter too much inside to out and catch the ball on the heel of the putter. The putt is hooked left. And, too, when hitting up on the ball there will be a natural deceleration of the putter at impact. Pendulums accelerate downward, not upward.

I prefer to hit a "light" ball, one that rolls over the very top of the grass. The grain of the green has less effect on a "light" ball. It rolls better on greens in all sorts of conditions—wet, bumpy, spiked and so on.

You get a "light" ball by hitting it at the very bottom of your forward swing. That is the essence of the pendulum stroke. *The clubhead is moving level with the ground—in the flat spot—at impact.*

However, the putter does not stay low throughout the stroke, and it shouldn't be forced to. The club wants to go up and down and should be allowed to do just that. But it wants to go up and down *on the same arc in both directions.*

How do you know where the bottom of your

A demonstration of how the arms should form a cradle when in putting address position. The idea is to keep your arms away from your body to promote a straight-line arms and shoulders stroke.

If you rock the "cradle" to the inside on the takeaway of the putting stroke, you will almost invariably rock it to the inside on the through-stroke. Such a stroke produces side-spin rather than perfect overspin, which is the ideal roll on the ball.

stroke is? Take your normal address position without a ball, and swing your putter as you do when actually hitting a putt. Notice where the blade just brushes the top of the grass. That's the bottom of your stroke. If you change ball-to-head alignment in your stance, your low spot will also change. Which brings me to the details of the address position.

At address: 10 fingers on and arms away

I prefer the 10-finger grip for putting. I think that when you have all the fingers on the club,

you have more control of it.

Set the club along the calluses of each hand, but just a tad more toward the palms. The thumbs are angled across the top of the handle.

The right hand is turned well to the right, the left hand is turned well to the left. It's basically the same fingernails-up grip used for chipping. The hands are directly opposed to each other; they are in balance.

Grip pressure is evenly distributed in the hands. Many golfers like to take one hand out of putting, usually the right hand. They worry that it will be too dominant in the stroke and change the swing path or the angle of the club-face. Thus, they apply a little more grip pressure with the left hand. But this isn't necessary if the grip is in balance in respect to their placement.

Some golfers putt with both arms fully extended at address. I think this is fine for taller players. For shorter persons, though, I think it is easier to putt with the arms bent at address. I bend my arms so they form a cradle, with the elbows pointing outward. It is very similar to the way I chip. Either way, be in balance. Keep both arms straight, or bent.

However, I am very much opposed to anyone putting with his arms up against the body. I find a lot of golfers doing this. It prohibits motion with the arms, creates tension, especially in the left arm, and promotes a wristy slapping of the ball; you want a swinging stroke.

I want everyone's arms to be *away from his body* so the arms can swing freely, without restrictions. The cradling of the arms that I use tends to keep the arms away from the body.

At address, *have the club on the same angle as your arms.* That is, the club is no more, or less, vertical than your arms. Neither is the club tilted to the left or right; your hands are on a line even with the ball, not ahead of or behind it. The best way to check this is to have a friend look at your address from directly behind, looking down the target line. (Or from in front, looking back from the target.) He should *not be able to see the handle of the club.*

It will be hidden by your arms (see illustration). You might also have a photograph taken that you can then use to check *all* your positions at address.

Even when watching your *stroke* from the same angle, the handle of the club should not be seen. That's because you will—or should—swing the *whole* club back and through, with the arms and shoulders and club moving as a single unit.

Put another way, your arms and shoulders form a triangle at address, just as they do when making the full swing. The club bisects the triangle. If you stand at the putt with your arms extended, the triangle will be narrower than the one for putters who bend their arms. But the triangle never changes its shape, and the club remains within the frame throughout the stroke.

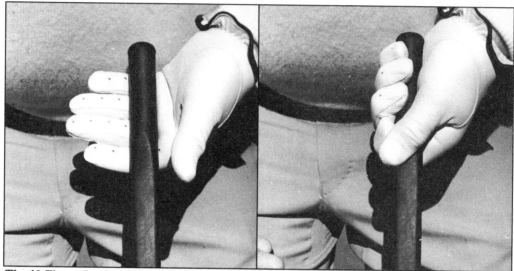

The 10-Finger Putting Grip: Club is set along jointure of palm and fingers, but slightly more toward palm. Palm faces up, and when the hand closes the thumb is angled across the handle of the club.

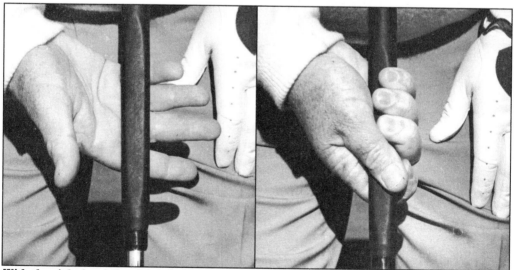

With the right hand the club is held more in the fingers. The hand is turned well to the right, under the handle, and the thumb is also angled across. Fingernails of both hands face up.

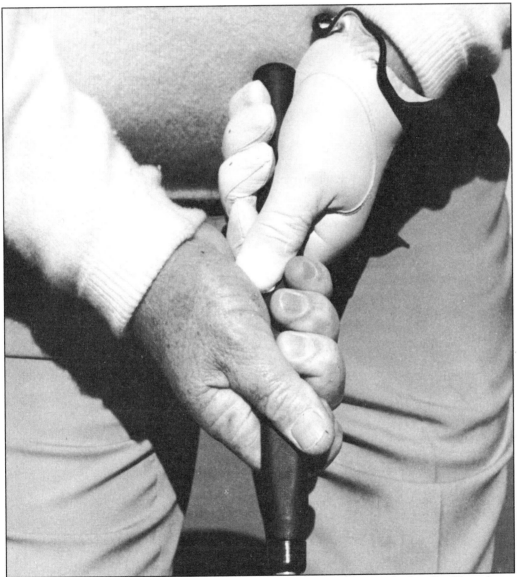

With completed grip the hands are exactly opposed in their angling on the handle. The grip promotes a stroke with no wrist action. Grip pressure is evenly distributed, no more exerted with the left hand than the right.

Stance and posture

As to ball-to-feet relationship in putting, and whether the stance should be open, closed or square, I will not be absolutely specific. Putting tends to be the most individualistic part of golf and particularly in these aspects.

My own putting technique follows fairly closely my overall swing concept. I play the ball off the left heel, and off the left side of my face. My eyes are directly over the back of the ball (and the target line). This way I can feel as though I am hitting underneath the ball.

I also like to be square at address. Both feet are at a 90-degree angle to the parallel line. The knees, hips and shoulders are parallel.

I recommend that everyone *take a little wider stance than usual when putting*, because in putting you want stability, not mobility. You don't want the head or trunk to move; only the shoulders and arms move.

In the full swing, one downside of a wide stance is the lack of mobility that can cause the head to move too much. But this won't happen in putting with a wide stance, because the swing is not big enough.

I think body weight should be concentrated on one side or the other, *and at least two-thirds on the weighted side*. I prefer the weight on the left side; it better suits the parallel stance. Even if you should use an open stance, you have the weight distributed on one side or the other.

Whichever side you choose, *the weight distribution should be constant during the entire stroke*. It must not shift from one side to the other.

Stand on the balls of your feet, bend only at the waist. Flex your knees, but not very much, to assure your back is straight.

Preputting

One big reason successful businessmen are successful is because they are always prepared before they make important decisions. They never go into a business meeting without all the information they can get their hands on. You should do the same thing when playing golf.

I realize that for most golfers the game is just that, a game, and I totally agree that they should first and foremost have fun at it, use the game as a break from more urgent responsibilities. But the truth of it is, golf is always more fun when we play it well. It follows then that before we start a round or get ready to play a single shot, we should be as well prepared as possible. In putting that involves many different things.

There's the general line of the putt to determine: is it going to go straight, or break to the right or left? Are you putting uphill or downhill, and how steep is the hill? Is the green running fast, slow, medium? Is there grain in the grass that will affect the roll of the ball? And, in respect to my number system for putting, what's the distance to the hole? That seems like a lot to do, but the process eventually becomes automatic and everything tends to meld into one activity.

Another reason golfers come up with the putting "yips" is that they are not sure of what they want to do with a putt, and when they get over the ball they panic. They've put unnecessary pressure on themselves. The golfer who knows what he wants to do with a putt in both the mechanics of the stroke and the line and speed of the green, doesn't feel the pressure of a competitive situation as much. It's not that he isn't aware of it, but he's better able to cope

The plumb-bob system to determine the general contour of the surface over which you are to putt. Hold your club a few feet in front of you, hanging vertically and centered on the ball. Look at the club with your dominant eye only, keeping the other eye closed.

with it because he's done his homework. This breeds the kind of confidence and comfort that allows the best possible execution of the stroke. Not every putt is going to go in, but the percentage of successes will surely be higher.

It may seem too time-consuming, all the pacing of footage, etc. But it promotes better golf, which means fewer strokes, and in the end speeds up play.

Reading the green

You should begin to get an idea of the overall contour of a green before you even step onto it. The long view from five or 10 yards away can be more revealing in this respect than the close-up. Once on the green, get low behind your ball and look for the contour between it and the hole; if there is contour, will it take your ball to the right or the left? I also like to use the plumb-bob method for this. To plumb-bob, hold the putter vertically in front of you and centered on your ball. Look at the club with only your dominant eye, closing the other eye. You should be able to see the *general* contour of the ground but not the refinements (see illustration).

Survey the ground between your ball and the hole from the side, which usually will show whether a putt is uphill or downhill and can also give you a sense of the arch or brow of a green.

Your feet are very sensitive and just by walking around on a green you can get a feel of whether you're going sidehill, uphill or downhill. Through your feet you can also get a feel for the speed of a green, how fast or slow it is running. Be alert to this sense. Additional feel for the speed of a green comes from watching the putts of playing partners and from your own experience after playing a hole or two.

Spotting the grain

The grain of the grass on a green is determined by the direction in which the blades are lying. If you're putting into the blade-tips there is more resistance to the ball than if it were rolling in the direction of the tips. If the blade-tips lie across your line of putt, the ball tends to roll toward them; when the tips lie to the left, expect the ball to roll in that direction to some extent. You read the grain a number of ways.

Grain is usually heavy on courses in mountain areas, and it usually runs away from the mountains. Grain is also prevalent in the South, where the greens are often Bermuda grass. It's a good idea to know which way is west because the grass generally grows in the direction of the setting sun. This is particularly important when playing on Bermuda grass, because it grows in the hotter climates and is more affected by the sun. This is a good tip when playing late in the day when the grass has grown some.

Look down the line of your putt, and if the grass appears shiny then you're going with the grain. If it appears dark, you're going against it.

The area of green around six feet or so of the hole is most important as regards reading the grain, because the ball is slowing down at this point and is then most affected by the grain. I must say, though, that if you roll the ball like I'm trying to get you to, on top of the grass lightly, grain will never greatly affect the roll of the ball.

Look for old ball marks on the green that leave a depression that can bump your ball off line. You're allowed to fix them.

Pinpoint target focus

You have looked over the terrain and made a decision on how you think the ball will roll in terms of speed and break. If it is a breaking putt and you figure the ball will break four inches to the left, pick a spot four inches to the right of the hole and putt straight to it. In this way, *every putt is essentially a straight putt* and you always make your normal stroke. You will not be tempted to hook or cut the ball to suit the contour of the green.

On short putts—12 feet and under—you can be more precise. So pick a spot. Focus on that spot and aim to hit it with the ball. Always focus on the smallest possible thing when putting. The smaller and more precise your target, the sharper it will be to you. This also helps your concentration; you create "tunnel vision" that blocks out peripheral distractions. It's another way of beating the putting "yips," too, because it helps deflect tension the competitive situation may be creating.

Some putting instruction says to pick a spot on the line of putt *before* the hole and hit to it. But I want distance to be the preeminent factor in putting, which is why you should find a spot on the *lip* of the cup and focus on it.

Rehearse with the practice stroke

You're now at the ball and just about ready to hit your putt. There is one more part of the pre-putt program, and it's one of the most important—the practice stroke or rehearsal. Everybody should always take at least three or four practice strokes, and they should be *exact simulations* of the stroke you will be using for the putt at hand. If you have a 12-footer, your practice strokes are for that length of putt!

One of my pet peeves is watching practice strokes where golfers take a huge, long stroke back and through. They say it's to relieve tension and it may do that, but it is not the stroke they're going to use and all they are doing is confusing the body. On the other hand, I love to see practice strokes where the player is swinging the club back and through with a nice pendulum motion, the same stroke he will be using just a few seconds later. That's a proper rehearsal—a dress rehearsal.

Why do we always hit a putt well the second time after missing it the first time? Because we now have a feel for the speed, as well as knowledge of the break. We don't get "overs" or "mulligans" on the putting green, so the only way to grasp some feeling for the stroke pace you need is to mimic the stroke you want *before* you hit the ball.

Nothing leaves a golfer so depleted spiritually as a three-putt green. You can recover from a poor drive or approach shot, but you can't from a three-putt.

SUCCESSFUL PUTTING IS NOT THREE-PUTTING. Your chances of three-putting are greatly reduced when you concentrate on the distance and an evenly paced stroke.

The Sand Game

An overview

I remember an instance on the tour when I holed out a bunker shot in which the ball rolled about 20 feet before going in. I didn't get much applause, because the gallery thought I missed the shot and just got lucky. But that's the way I played it. A rolling ball always has a better chance of going into the hole than one that is bouncing or spinning. Which is to say, I am not interested in trying to spin the ball out of the sand any more than I am when playing the pitch shot.

In fact, in my system, bunker play and pitching are very similar in technique as well as philosophy. The swing is identical. The differences are a matter of degree more than basic technique. In the bunker the stance is slightly open, and you want to hit *well* behind the ball for shots of any length. And the swing is between two and three times as hard. What you must remember about the standard greenside bunker shot is that *the sand takes the ball out.* The clubhead never touches the ball. The sign of a properly played bunker shot is when sand is knocked onto the green, along with the ball.

Widen your chances

Most golfers know they must hit behind the ball in the sand. But the considerable troubles many have with this shot come from not hitting far enough behind it and, at the same time, trying to "cut" the ball out with a wide-open clubface and a very vertical, outside-to-in swing path. That has been the "traditional" way to play out of greenside traps—nipping the ball and putting a lot of backspin, or cut-spin, on it. But that shot takes many hours of practice, years really, to master.

At that, you need just the right texture of sand—a little on the firm side—and the ball sitting right up on top of it. The margin for error is not great enough. More often than he cares to remember, the golfer trying this low-percentage technique doesn't hit behind the ball at all. Rather, he hits only the ball—"blades" it or hits it thin—and lines it over the green.

The other common error is to hit too far behind the ball in an effort to scoop it out. Now the club digs in too far behind the ball and it is "dumped"—it stays in the bunker or just doesn't go far enough.

The three priorities

There are three primary goals with any greenside bunker shot. In order of priority they are (1) Get Out—of the bunker, (2) Get On—the green, (3) Get Close—to the hole. By giving yourself the biggest possible margin for error, you are always going to get out of the sand, usually on the green, and more often close to the hole.

The margin derives from *always hitting four inches behind the ball for shots of all lengths.* The more consistent your contact with the sand, the more consistent the results of these shots. This bunker shot requires less practice for one thing, and basically produces the same spin on the ball all the time. It is true underspin, not sidespin. As with the pitch shot from grass, the ball will take a short bounce and start rolling. There will be no skidding effect. When you hit too close to the ball in the sand, it tends to come out much faster, take a longer bounce and skid. A skidding ball is a ball out of control.

Clear the sand box

In teaching the basic greenside sand shot, I have my students imagine the back of the ball sitting in the middle of an eight-inch square box. I ask them to clear that whole box out of the bunker. The clubhead enters the sand four inches behind the ball and exits about two to three inches in front of it. The "divot" is also the width of the box, because the sand explodes out to the sides as well as ahead. It's basically a square divot. The more rectangular the divot, the worse the shot. It means you've cut the ball out instead of blasting it.

The divot is not especially deep. I don't teach a very steep downstroke for the bunker shot, or deep penetration of the sand. The ball is 1.68 inches in diameter, and it is usually sitting about halfway into the sand, so the club doesn't have to go more than an inch to an inch and a half into the sand in order to get under the ball

without touching it. The club is on a descending plane when it enters the sand, but levels out so that *the flat spot, or bottom of the arc, is directly under the ball.*

To repeat, hitting at least four inches behind the ball in the sand provides a margin of safety, a cushion against hitting the shot thin. If you make a three-inch error and hit only an inch behind it—and that's a big error—you're still going to come up with a reasonably effective shot. The ball will go a little farther and faster, but it will probably stop faster. If the error is two or three inches in the other direction, and you hit six inches behind the ball, the club will still get under the ball and knock it out of the bunker; this ball probably won't carry as far, but it will roll farther than normal.

In short, the misses are more forgiving.

Grip and address

The sand, of course, is going to offer more resistance to the passage of the clubhead than grass, so your grip pressure should be a little firmer than normal. Naturally, you maintain that same pressure throughout the swing. Otherwise, use your standard grip—interlocking, overlapping.

Ball alignment

The ball is played off the left heel for all sand shots. The angle of the swing arc changes for different textures of sand but the adjustments are made with the distribution of weight at address, not ball-to-feet alignment. I will point out those differences further on. At this point I want to present the basic sand-shot technique.

Address for the sand shot: Ball is always played off left heel. Weight distribution varies depending on slope of lie. Width of stance is only slightly wider than normal, and feet are not dug too deeply into the sand.

The stance is only slightly open in relation to the target, because the swing is basically the same as for all other standard golf shots. However, the hands cock up a little sooner.

The turning and straightening of left side brings handle of club onto the parallel line, and the clubhead from inside to square at impact to create the underhand-toss motion.

The turning, or rotation, of the right side brings the club in toward the body to create a standard hook-type swing path. The club is on the parallel-to-target line.

Hands recock quickly after impact, the clubhead getting above the hands and swinging out toward the target. At completion of follow-through you should be directly facing the target.

Hold inner half of clubhead directly above point in sand where you want club to enter, generally four inches behind ball. The heel of club is set low, the toe high. Club cannot be grounded in a bunker.

Staying mobile

You want to set your feet in the sand so they are essentially level with the bottom of the ball. Thus, they will not be as deep as most golfers have them. I don't believe in digging down into the sand as far as you can go. Neither do I think the stance should be extra wide; just a touch more than normal will do.

The reasoning for both positions is the same —greater mobility. You want lower-body motion in the sand-shot swing, a rotation of the hips. If the stance is too wide and you've buried your feet in the sand, the tendency is to use too much upper-body motion and slide laterally. You want no sideway movement of the upper body when playing out of sand, just as you want very little with any other shot.

The stance is open about 15 or 20 degrees so you are facing the hole. Weight distribution is to the left, at a ratio of 60-40 (see illustrations).

Use the inside half of the clubface

For the bunker shot, you want to use the strongest portion of the club, which is from the heel out to the middle of the blade. So when addressing the ball, keep the *heel down* and the *toe up.* You get this position by pressing the heels of your hands as low as you can at address.

The idea is to have the inside half of the clubface hit into the sand. This will turn the toe of the club in and create a hooking-type action on the ball. If the toe of the club—its weakest part —should hit the sand first, the clubface will slow down considerably and twist open. Not enough sand will be taken out.

You want to do everything you can at address to feel you can *hook the sand shot.*

Aim the inside half of the clubface at the target.

Normally, the center of the clubface is aimed at the target, which sets it square. With only the inner half aimed at the target, the face will be fractionally open to the target as well as the body, enough to compensate for the open stance.

Hold the inner half of the clubhead directly above the point in the sand where you want the club to enter. Don't block from your vision the point of contact, as many golfers tend to do, by holding the clubhead right behind—and above —the ball. (Remember, you're not allowed to ground your club at address.)

Inside-to-out swing path

The swing for the bunker shot is essentially the same as that for standard shots. It is the basic inside-to-out path.

—The hands cock up at the start of the backswing so the head of the club gets above the handle as soon as possible.

—The rotation of the right side brings the club in toward the body on the backswing. The turning and straightening of the left side bring the hands and the handle of the club onto the parallel line on the downswing and create the underhand-toss motion.

Both hands recock quickly after impact. The club points out to the target, and at the completion of the follow-through you are facing the target. The sand flies well out on to the green and directly at the target.

Keep the butt of the club as low as possible throughout the swing.

To someone standing behind the player this may not look like a hook-type swing. But the club swings inside to out *in relation to the body.* It swings parallel in relation to the target line.

'Walking the plank'

There is a drill I use to teach the parallel-line swing action. A long wooden board or plank is set in the sand aimed at the target and sunk down so the top is even with the surface of the trap. Balls are hit off the plank, which is covered with a pile of sand about an inch thick, six to seven inches long and as wide as the plank. The plank is a guide for the parallel line of the club through impact.

Playing a ball off a plank set in the sand is a drill to practice swinging the club along the parallel line. The swing is the same, with the club hitting four inches behind ball and directly along the line of the plank.

The idea is to knock all the sand off the board with each shot. You *hit the board four inches behind the ball* and as hard as you want with the back of the flange. I will often put some paint on the board so students can tell where the club is making contact with the board. They are amazed when the ball flies up nice and soft, with true underspin. The same principle is at work as for the pitch shot from hardpan that I described in the chapter on pitching.

Getting the distance

I have said that for bunker shots you swing harder than for pitches. That is obviously because sand is so much more resistant than grass. Here again, there is a general ratio. It is approximately 3 to 1. If you have a 20-yard explosion shot from a bunker, take a swing that emulates at least a 40-yard pitch from grass.

As I've said, you hit four inches in the sand behind the ball for all shots, no matter the length. That should never vary. Some people advocate hitting one inch behind the ball for a 30-yard shot, two inches behind for a 20-yard shot and so on. But that breeds inconsistency; it's harder to control than the length and speed of a swing. *To control distance you change only the length and speed of the swing.*

It has been my observation that most golfers tend to underswing out of the bunkers. I think it's because they try to be too cute, to do too much with the shot, and make short, jerky swings. The rule of thumb is *fit the length of the swing to the length of the shot,* using the 3-to-1 ratio.

Whatever the length of the swing make it firm, and be sure the *rhythm and pace are equal on both sides.*

People are amazed that the ball comes off the plank just as high and soft as if the ball was being played out of the sand or even grass.

The shot played off the plank is the best possible illustration of how hitting in the flat spot works in the sand.

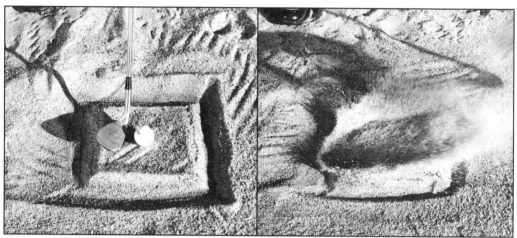

A sand-shot drill: Ball sits in middle of an eight-inch square box. Club enters sand at back of box and explodes the entire length and width of it.

Knock the sand out of the bunker

An important key to the success of bunker shots of any length is the uncocking, or release, of the wrists and hands. The club has to keep moving through so enough sand is knocked up and out to take the ball forward. You don't want to stop the club's progress by blocking the release of the hands. Complete your swing every time!

The sound of a good bunker shot is a short, solid thump.

Adjustments for texture

The shots I have been describing are for the kind of sand that is most prevalent on golf courses. It has a certain density we're all familiar with. It is not too powdery, not too tightly packed or heavy. But there are some different sand textures that need special attention.

As I said earlier, for all bunker shots the ball is played off the left heel. But when the texture of the sand is different from normal, there are some other adjustments that must be made, too.

When the sand has been soaked by rain and is tightly packed and hard, I recommend using a pitching wedge to get more of a cutting action. Also, you want a steeper swing arc—a more sharply descending blow—to promote that cutting action. You achieve this by opening your stance and with a greater distribution of weight to the left side; the ratio is 75-25. You will be leaning more to the left than normal.

If you need fairly significant distance, open the blade a little to put more bounce on the flange.

When the sand is wet but tilled up, it is very heavy and resists the club a lot. You have to swing harder and keep the club going, so it is

The divot is not especially deep. The important thing is to clear the width of the box as much as the length.

important that you have a firm hold on it. Use the sand wedge, but in order to get sufficient cutting action, lean your body more to the left at address. This promotes a steeper swing arc.

Out of powdery new sand or very deep sand, the ball is probably sitting a little below the surface. Thus, the first goal is to get the clubhead under the ball. Use the sand wedge, and again, concentrate more weight on the left side; it needn't be a lot—about 60-40 will do.

However, if the ball is sitting on top of this relatively soft sand, open the face of the sand wedge a little more and *lean to the right* to prohibit excessive digging.

Whenever you get into a bunker, get a feel for the texture of the sand through your feet as you take your address position. This helps you *know* the texture of the sand; it gives you a sense of how hard you must hit the shot.

The buried lie

When you have what is sometimes called a "fried egg," a ball plugged or buried in the sand, use the pitching wedge. The sand wedge is designed to prohibit cutting too deeply into the sand, but when the ball is buried that is exactly what you have to do. Remember, the ball is 1.68 inches in diameter, so if it is buried, say, another half an inch, you have to get the club at least two to two and a half inches into the sand to get beneath it. Because the flange of the pitching wedge has much less bounce and the leading edge is sharp, this club provides the kind of cutting action needed.

For a buried-lie shot of 10 yards or less, play with the face square to dig a little deeper and minimize the amount of roll after the ball lands. When more than 10 yards, open the face a little to get a slightly more shallow penetration of the sand and more roll.

The swing is essentially the same as for the standard bunker shot, although you must hit behind the crater in which the ball is sunk.

You want a slightly more descending blow, so at address lean to the left with body weight distributed about 70-30 to promote a more vertical swing arc.

A follow-through isn't essential. Don't worry about getting the club out of the sand, just try to get it past the ball. This is not a shot you can expect much from. It is a shot where the first priority for all sand play is especially emphasized. GET THE BALL OUT OF THE BUNKER. To that end, take the easiest, safest route, *even if you have to shoot away from the hole.* For instance, if you have a high lip to get over, look for a lower portion. And if the hole is cut in a narrow section of the green, shoot for the wider part.

Unlevel lies in the sand

The basic technique for playing shots off unlevel lies is the same from grass or sand. It has mainly to do with the address position. However, there are a few things about playing from the sand that are different. I'll deal with those differences here, and talk about playing off sloping ground in general in the following chapter.

Go with the flow

The first rule for playing off uphill and downhill lies in the sand (and on the grass) is to set your body and the club at right angles to the slope. In other words, if you're playing uphill your body tilts to the right and when playing downhill it tilts to the left. You're leaning in one direction or the other relative to a normal, level lie, but you are in effect level in respect to the contour of the terrain from which you're actually playing (see illustration).

Too many golfers stand too upright for this shot instead of conforming the body to the lay of the land. Thus, on the uphillers they drive the club too deeply into the sand and don't knock enough sand out of the bunker; the ball comes up far short of target. On downhillers they fail to get the club deep enough into the sand.

You don't fight against nature, you go with it. The idea is to be able to take your standard swing, but have the club moving along the slope. It's done at address by *leaning your body and concentrating your weight on the lower side of the slope*. When going uphill you lean to the right and have more weight on your right side. It is just the opposite when going downhill—lean left, weight left.

When the *uphill* slope is especially steep, I

Playing the uphill lie from the sand (or turf) requires tilting your body to the right so it

Setting up your body at address to lean away from the slope is designed to prevent driving

conforms with the lie. The spine should be at a 90-degree angle or right angle to the slope.

the clubhead into the face of it. The clubhead swings along the line of the slope throughout the swing. The ball tends to fly higher than usual, and stop quickly after landing.

The downhill lie is hardest of the unlevel lies to play well, especially from the sand. Tilt your body to the left to conform with the slope, and make a steeper backswing than normal to assure hitting deep enough into sand behind the ball.

Keep your weight on your left side throughout the swing for this shot, and be sure you begin the release of your wrists and hands early enough in the downswing. Aim to hit at least four inches behind the ball. If lie is extra steep, use your pitching wedge.

The danger with this shot is not digging deeply enough, catching the ball too cleanly and knocking it over the green.

Shots from downhill lies do not get much height, and the ball will always have run. Don't expect to get close to the hole; your main concern is to get somewhere on the green.

suggest you open the blade of the club a little to further prevent a digging action.

The hardest of these two shots, by far, is the downhiller. The natural tendency is for the clubhead to slide along the slope and not get deep enough into the sand. This shot can be easily "bladed," the ball coming out too fast and low to stay on the green. The swing arc must be steeper to insure that the club gets down and in. You can use the sand wedge, but to get more cutting action square the blade at address. However, when the slope is particularly severe it is a good idea to use the pitching wedge to get a sharper leading edge. Remember, you must get the clubhead under the ball.

A different flight, a different distance

Even when you make adjustments at address for playing uphill and downhill shots, the ball will have a different trajectory than usual. A ball played from an uphill lie will go higher and for that reason will stop faster. But you can't and shouldn't do anything about that. It's the nature of the shot. It will not go as far as a normal sand shot, and you have to judge how much harder to swing to get the distance needed.

On the downhiller, the ball is never going to get very high in the air, no matter what you do. It is just about always going to come out low and fast and with a lot of run. Unless you have a lot of green to the hole, you don't stand much chance of getting the ball close. In fact, you can easily run this shot off the green on the other side and into trouble.

On those occasions when you can't wisely shoot at the pin, I recommend playing away from it. This can change the angle of the lie and the path of the swing to where you can end up playing from less-severely sloped ground. Now you can hit a more conventional, easier shot and be fairly sure of getting the ball on the green. At least you'll be putting. It's a common-sense way out of trouble that avoids the dreaded double bogey.

Sidehill in the sand

When the ball is above or below your feet, there is not much you can do to conform your body to the terrain. You can't lean back from the ball when it's above your feet, and you don't want to lean too much forward when it's below them.

When the ball is above your feet the tendency is to stand too far from the ball and make a kind of baseball swing—a flatter than normal swing path. The ball tends to be pulled or hooked to the left of the target. You want to swing along the slope of the ground as much as possible, so the swing for this lie is going to be a little flatter than usual in any case. But to reduce the pulling-hooking action of the ball, choke down on the grip so you stand a bit closer to the ball and can make a more vertical swing.

To further compensate for the natural tendency to hit this shot to the left, aim more to the right so you swing up the slope; and open the clubface slightly more than normal.

When the ball is below your feet, the tendency is to get too close to the ball. So, hold the club at the end of the handle to be sure you don't crowd the ball. The swing path should definitely be along the slope. Therefore, open the stance a little, and play the ball more toward the left heel. It may appear that the ball is too far forward, but only because of the body's relationship to the target.

Aim to the left of the target so that you are swinging up the slope and can make solid contact with the ball. Keep the clubface square.

The ball tends to fly to the right from this lie, but your positioning at address should put the ball on the target.

The long explosion

Most golfers are in a real quandary about how to deal with a sand shot from a distance that seems to be out of range for the regular explosion, yet is not far enough from the green to be played like a fairway shot. Just about everyone prefers to explode the ball but doesn't know how to get the distance.

First of all, you have to know how far you can hit the ball from the grass with the sand wedge. Then go by the numbers. The rule of thumb is, *if the farthest you can hit the ball from the grass is 60 yards, then you can only hit it 20 yards from the sand.* The ratio is approximately 3 to 1. That makes your decision easy when you have a long explosion shot. Step off your yardage. If you're outside your sand-wedge range, so be it. Always take the easiest and safest way out.

But you can still play an explosion-type shot with a sand wedge or pitching wedge, and hit four inches behind the ball! The swing mechanics are the same as for the standard pitch shot. The key is to *open the blade much more than normal and swing harder.*

By opening the blade at address, the bounce on the club is increased. This keeps the blade from digging and creates more of a blasting effect. More sand will come out to carry the ball the distance. The farther you hit the sand, the farther the ball goes.

The long explosion: Hit about four inches behind ball, with blade of club opened slightly to avoid digging too deeply. Play ball from same position as for standard shots, off left heel, with weight evenly balanced and feet not too deep.

Stance should be slightly open, and backswing to inside, in relation to the body with a good turn of shoulders and hips. Downswing begins with a straightening of left leg that creates a shift of weight to the left and initiates the underhand-toss motion.

Hands should definitely release early for the long explosion. The farther forward you hit the sand, the farther the ball will go.

For the long explosion, figure to hit the ball one-third as far as you would when playing from the grass.

From the fairway bunkers

From fairway bunkers there is no question of whether or not you can explode the ball. You *must hit the ball first.*

This is not as difficult a shot as people make it. Let's talk about the priorities first. The cardinal rule, again, is Get Out, get the ball back on grass where you can do more with it. Don't try to be a hero with a "career shot" of 180 yards or whatever that must carry other bunkers and/or water, unless you have no choice. If you're 1 down with one hole left in the match, give it a go. Otherwise, play smart.

The fairway bunker shot isn't hard if all you want to do is to move the ball well forward into a decent position for the next shot. Very often these bunkers have a lip that must be carried from close up, so make sure the club you use has enough loft to clear it. If it is not enough club to reach the green, so be it. There is nothing worse than hitting the ball solidly and driving it right into the lip, or burying it in the face of the bunker. That spells double bogey or worse. You are always better off hitting the ball out and into a scoring area.

If you have 175 yards to the green, let's say, and there is a good-sized lip on the bunker, and there are bunkers guarding the front of the green, take a 7- or 8-iron if that will assure clearing the lip. You can't reach the green with either of those clubs no matter how well you hit them, but neither will you stick the ball in the lip of the trap, nor put it in one of the greenside bunkers. You'll be well short of the green but in the fairway with a relatively simple pitch. Now that you know how to pitch, you can save your par; or do no worse than make a bogey. You don't want to go from trouble to trouble. I see that happening far too often.

This is not to say you can't or should never try for the green from a fairway trap. But you try only when the conditions are very favorable; for instance, when the ball is sitting on top of firmly packed sand that provides good footing, the lip of the bunker is not very high, and you are far enough back to clear it with the club needed to carry all the way to the green. Now go for it!

Of course, whether you're going for the green or laying up short in the fairway, you still have to make good contact with the ball. The key is to swing within yourself.

Sidehill explosion (ball below feet): The ball almost invariably flies out to the right from this type of lie, so be sure to aim more left than normally. Also, the tendency is to stand too close to the ball, and fall toward the ball during the downswing.

It is important to swing the club along the slope of the ground. Therefore, open the stance a bit more and play ball more toward left heel.

The club may swing a bit farther away from your body than for standard shots, but it will be in conjunction with the angle of the slope.

The fairway bunker shot is never exploded; it is a fairway shot from sand. You must stand tall at address, with a bit more weight on the left side. Stance is slightly open, to encourage slightly more upright swing plane.

Aim to hit the center-back of the ball—just below its equator—to avoid hitting into sand behind it. The blow is more vertical—you do not hit it in the flat spot.

Feet are not sunk deeply into sand so they can be mobile in the swing action. Ball is played off the left heel.

Fairway bunker shots will have a lower trajectory than normal so be sure to use club with enough loft to clear lip.

Stand tall, swing three-quarter

First of all, in addressing these shots, have a little more weight on the left side and *keep that left side tall and firm.* Open your stance fractionally. Both these factors will promote a somewhat more vertical swing.

Secondly, set your feet comfortably into the sand but not so deep that they are stuck. Even though you're not going to make a full swing here, you do want some mobility.

Position the ball normally, off the left heel. Open the clubface slightly, and *set the clubhead at the ball's equator*—hold it at the back-center of the ball, not down near the bottom. This helps prevent hitting into the sand behind the ball; you very definitely do not want to hit fat from a fairway bunker. You may hit the ball a bit thin once in a while, but the ball will go forward. Fat gets you nowhere.

Standing tall at address helps you get a full arm extension. It is especially important that the left arm be fully extended; you can even lock the elbow. This is also to prevent hitting a fat shot.

Keep the toe of the club up, the heel down. Full arm extension and pressing the heels of the hands downward aid in this.

You want to get the club underneath the ball, just as with a standard shot. But in this case the downswing is a little more vertical, and you hit the ball at the very bottom of the downstroke, *not in the flat spot.*

Expect these shots to have a little lower trajectory than usual, because every mechanic I've described is predicated on hitting the ball cleanly and getting it out of the bunker.

To repeat, you should be trying primarily for good contact with the ball. To further that end, *the swing should be no more than three-quarter pace.* If your normal 5-iron goes 150 yards, make a swing that will hit it 130 or 120 yards. Distance is a secondary goal to getting the ball back in play.

Go 'Baffler'™

I am just about entirely opposed to using a fairway wood out of a fairway bunker—I mean a 3- or 4-wood. You need absolutely perfect conditions—the ball sitting up on the very top of the sand and a bunker with no lip.

On the other hand, the utility club called The "Baffler," which is a wood club, is excellent for long fairway bunker shots.

The Baffler, which has two raised runners on the sole, is used just the same as a sand wedge. The runners prevent the club from digging into the sand. The only way you can miss a shot with the club is to top the ball. So you can play my basic sand shot with it from a fairway bunker, except you hit between two and four inches behind the ball, and fly it up to 175 yards. It has the loft of about a 5-wood. (The Baffler is also an excellent club for playing out of deep grass.)

Most people tend to make a short, fast swing in a fairway bunker, probably out of anxiety or a feeling that they must hit the ball hard. But if you maintain a good posture at address—stand tall—and think in terms of a three-quarter swing and just getting the ball back into play, it won't be a great problem.

The "Baffler," the only wooden-headed club you should use for a fairway bunker shot.

Shotmaking

Playing in the wind—go easier

When I first went to Texas to attend the University of Houston and play on the golf team, I got a chance to play with Byron Nelson. Of course, I had heard a lot about Nelson but had never really seen him play. One of the first things I noticed was that every time he played into the wind his hands went down on the grip at least half an inch, and he narrowed his stance. He also swung the club much easier. He was not the kind of person who would say, "I play this hole with a drive and a wedge." He played a hole with the clubs that were necessary according to the circumstances of the moment. He didn't care if it was a drive and a 7-iron one day, a drive and a 2-iron the next. He wanted to make sure his swing was always under control.

Another time I played with Nelson in the wind, at the Colonial Invitational soon after I started on the tour, and he said, "I don't care about elevation very much. I care about hitting the ball squarely."

The point is that into the wind you swing a little easier so you don't get as much spin on the ball. That way the wind has less influence on its flight, and you don't have to worry about elevation. It's not necessary to "knock the ball down," by making a swing different from normal just to hit the ball lower. You use your normal swing pattern so you strike the ball consistently. Only the swing pace differs. You can control swing pace better than swing pattern. Apply the three-gear concept.

The validity of this approach to playing into the wind, or in whatever direction it's blowing, is proved out at the British Open. The wind is always a big factor on the links-type courses on which that championship is played, and the last half a dozen or so winners have been high-ball hitters. I'm referring especially to Jack Nicklaus and Tom Watson and Seve Ballesteros. They don't try to beat the ball down when they play in the wind, they just hit the ball squarely.

A minor adjustment

The only adjustment in technique I use when playing into the wind, and usually only with the driver, is to play the ball a touch more forward in the stance. I want to hit the ball with the swing rising just a bit at impact, so I am not putting as much underspin on the ball.

Good wind players don't tee the ball lower when going into the wind; they don't want to pinch the ball and get an upshooting trajectory that will hang in the air and roll not an inch. If anything, they tee the ball higher. They want to put less underspin on the ball with a swing in which the club is rising at impact. The ball gets up, but has the kind of spin that tumbles it over in a forward direction. When it lands it jumps ahead and gets a good roll.

When I first began playing on the tour with Jack Nicklaus, he outdrove me downwind by up to 100 yards. But into the wind I could drive up with him and sometimes past him. That was because he was then hitting the ball not only high but with a lot of underspin. It was a riser, or upshooter, that the wind held back. But he strikes the ball differently now, more the way I've been discussing in this book, and he has become much more effective in the wind. That's one reason why he has played so much better in recent years in Florida where the wind is strong and steady.

With the wind, take full swing

Golfers don't worry nearly as much about playing with the wind at their backs as they do when it's in their faces, especially when hitting their drivers. Nature is their best-buddy then, and is going to add some distance. But you can help yourself a little more in this situation by *hitting the ball a little harder with maximum power, but still under control.*

The harder you hit a golf ball the more underspin you put on it, so the higher it goes. You want more height going downwind not because the wind will carry the ball farther but because the wind tends to take the spin off it and knock it down. Therefore, the higher you hit the ball, the longer it will stay in the air...and the farther it will carry.

There is no significant mechanical adjustment to get the ball higher. Just hit it a bit harder. However, as I've pointed out

throughout this book but can't say too often, you hit harder by increasing the *overall pace of the swing.* You don't make a downswing that is faster than the backswing; the pace of *all* golf swings must be even from beginning to end.

Remember, you make a full swing going downwind, a three-quarter swing going into the wind.

In a crosswind—go with the flow

Wind blowing across your target line tends to take spin off the ball and push it in the direction it is blowing. That's a very acceptable situation. I don't advise the average golfer to attempt counteracting a crosswind by trying to hook a ball into a left-to-right breeze, or slice one into a right-to-left wind. That's stuff better left to professionals and very low-handicap golfers who play and practice every day and have a lot of control over their swings. However, use your imagination and play to your strength. If you naturally hit a draw or hook, then you can work a ball into the wind.

As a general rule, under crosswind conditions play your normal shot and always aim it so you use the "fat" side of the fairway or green. That is, if the wind is blowing left to right when you're hitting a driver from the tee, aim up the left side of the fairway. Now you have the entire width of the fairway to work with as the wind moves the ball to the right.

When playing an approach shot to the green, and the wind is blowing from right to left, start your shot at the right side of the green so you have the entire width of the green to work with. You should *always aim approach shots within the parameters of the putting surface.* Then, if the wind doesn't move the ball as much as expected, you will still have it somewhere on the green.

Never put yourself in a position where a straight ball gets you into trouble. For example, if the hole is cut in the right side of the green, with the wind blowing right to left, you should not aim to the right of the green expecting the wind to bring the ball into the pin. There is probably a bunker to the right, and if the wind doesn't move the ball, you're in it. But even if there is no bunker, chipping or pitching is more difficult from the side of the green closest to the hole. At most, aim at the right side of the green. If the wind doesn't move the ball, that's where you'll end up. If the wind does move it, you will still be putting. It may be a long putt, but that's better than playing out of trouble.

In other words, let the wind be your friend; use it as it is, go with its flow.

Club selection in the wind

Obviously the distance to be covered and how far you hit the ball under normal conditions are the first considerations in club selection when playing in the wind. But to them must be added the kind of swing you should make when going downwind or upwind.

INTO THE WIND you are going to swing easier, about 10 to 25 percent easier—remember, it's a three-quarter swing—so if you hit your 5-iron 150 yards on a calm day, for a shot of that length into the wind you take one more club—a 4-iron. It is not a completely cut-and-dry number decision, though. If the wind is exceptionally strong in your face, you may need a 3-iron. That is a matter of personal judgment. But the basic premise should be, *more is always better!* Probably 99 percent of golf shots that end up in trouble have not gone far enough! Especially approach shots. There is almost in-variably more trouble in front of a green than behind it.

WITH THE WIND you generally take one less club than usual for the distance and make a full swing. You can go two clubs down when the wind is particularly strong at your back. Always use the club you can, or should, hit fullest!

Club selection for *CROSSWIND* shots is pretty much similar to that for playing into the wind. Use one more club than normal for the distance, and make a three-quarter swing to keep the ball as low as possible. The less you get the ball up into the air, the less chance of it getting away from you. Don't get fancy. Remember, a solid hit is always better and more under control.

Swinging in the rain

When playing in any kind of foul weather, it is very important to maintain a basic principle that has been projected throughout this book. Which is, keep control of your swing; maintain your balance so you body doesn't waver in the wind and you won't slip when it's wet.

If you're swinging on slippery ground, the tendency is to become tentative and stiffen up; you worry about losing your footing. But *a rigid body is more apt to lose its balance than one that is relaxed.* What you have to do is play easier. Take 10 percent off your swing. And don't hurry! No one is ever comfortable playing in the rain. The urge is to rush the play and get back under the umbrella. But if you're out there, you've obviously committed yourself to the situation so make the best of it. You do that by not playing any faster than normal. Only when there is lightning in the sky do you rush...off the course.

Otherwise, be alert to the fact that rain makes the air heavier. For that reason, and also because you are going to be swinging a little easier, take more club to play an approach shot than you would under ordinary circumstances.

I think my swing concept is especially effective in the rain because the tendency is to hit the ball cleanly. The golfers who take big divots are the ones who get "squirters," shots that are out of control, because there is a much greater chance of moisture getting in between the clubface and ball at impact. With my swing you can nip the ball off the grass.

Playing the unlevel lies

In the chapter on bunker play, I discussed most of the fundamentals for playing from hilly lies. The same principles apply when playing off grass, but I'll repeat them here and add a few things that are especially pertinent to this situation.

First of all, you're very susceptible to a loss of balance when playing off unlevel lies, so all these shots should be played with *no more than a three-quarter-pace swing.*

Just as importantly, and this will also help retain balance, FOR UPHILL AND DOWN-HILL LIES set the angle of your body at address so it conforms to the tilt of the ground. In effect, this puts you level with the ball so you're addressing it at the correct 90-degree angle to the ground.

There is an image I use in teaching this. Visualize the letter T standing upside down on the ground. The angle at which it stands is the same your body should take.

When *PLAYING UPHILL* you want to be leaning to the right at the same angle as the slope of the ground, so concentrate more of your weight on the right leg. This will promote a low-to-high sweeping motion of the club, a swing path that follows the slope of the ground and prevents the club from digging too deeply into the hill before, or after, impact. That is what you most want to avoid on this shot— "sticking your pick," as the saying goes, which means the flow of the club through the shot is stopped.

Shots off an UPHILL LIE are going to go higher than normal. Figure the additional height into your club selection (along with the three-quarter swing you're going to make). In general, this means taking at least one more club than normal. The natural ball flight will be from straight to a draw.

THE DOWNHILL SHOT is one of the hardest in the game to get a real good result—off the grass just as much as in a bunker. With this shot more than any other, you want to simply get the ball to a place where the next shot gives you a chance to do well. You shouldn't try any heroics playing downhill. The ball is never going to get very high in the air—it's going to fly lower and faster than any other shot you hit, even if you strike it well. If it's a particularly long approach shot and the slope is especially steep, you can't figure on carrying the ball to the green. Look for the safest landing area in the fairway or the biggest part of the green, and play to it.

I don't want to be completely discouraging, though. The ball can be hit decently from this type of lie.

Once again, angle your body at address to conform with the slope of the ground, in this case by concentrating your weight on the left side.

With a severe lie, you should also play the

ball back toward the right foot an inch or two more than usual. Otherwise, the lean of the body at address will suffice.

Open your stance slightly to promote a more vertical swing. You need a steeper downswing path to hit this shot.

Use at least one club *less* than normal to be sure you have enough loft to get the ball up as much as possible. The usual flight from this lie is straight to fade; go with it, don't try to hook the ball.

Finally, on downhillers take a firmer grip; with the hands kind of "frozen" on the club, you have a better chance of pinching the ball and getting it in the air. Hitting the ball with a little more of a descending blow puts more underspin on the ball, which helps it to rise after its low-starting trajectory.

When the ball is on a *SIDEHILL ABOVE YOUR FEET*, the first thing you want to do is choke down on the grip a couple of inches. This prevents you from getting too far away from the ball at address, the common tendency, which promotes a swing path that is too flat or horizontal and brings a hooking or pulling action. You will still be swinging the club to the inside along the slope, and this tends to produce a straight-to-draw trajectory. To neutralize this, open the clubface a little more at address.

When the ball is on a *SIDEHILL BELOW THE FEET*, concentrate a little more weight on the left foot at address to promote a vertical takeaway that follows the slope as much as possible.

Hold the club at full length, open the stance slightly to promote a vertical swing path and aim just a touch left of your target. The path of the swing will be slightly outside to in, in relation to the target line but *inside to out in relation to your body*.

Most people say you will slice the ball off this lie, but I totally disagree with that. If you are addressing the ball with the heel of the club down and the toe up, as I teach for all shots except the chip, the heel of the club is going to hit the ground first and turn the toe inward or closed. Thus, the ball tends to go straight, and you can even get a little draw.

Managing Your Game

Club selection—know your yardage

As I've pointed out often throughout this book, distance is very important to my conception of how to play consistently good golf. The primary goal when playing pitch shots, chip shots or long putts is to stop the ball right beside the hole. With the longer approach shots you can't be quite that good on average, but you can hit the ball pin high—even with the hole to one side of it or the other.

When you're on the green and pin-high five yards to either side of the hole, you have a 15-foot putt. But if you're five yards wide *and* five yards *short* of the hole, you have about a 21-foot putt. That's why I stress getting the right distance and think that pinpoint aiming is a secondary issue. Not only are there more payoffs from having the distance, it is easier on your mind and body. Precision aiming as a first priority produces more tension than just trying to hit the ball squarely and get the correct distance.

It follows then that you have to know the distance from your ball to the target for shots that can reach the green. That information is easier to come by now than it was in the past. Just about all golf courses have some sort of markers placed 150 yards from the greens on the par-4 and par-5 holes, and many courses are providing even more elaborate information. A lot of them offer scorecards with hole diagrams on which the yardages from a number of points on each hole are designated—184 yards from the front edge of a fairway bunker, 137 yards from a water sprinkler in the middle of the fairway, and so on.

All this is very helpful but is misleading to, or is being misused by, many average golfers. With 170 yards to the green from a sprinkler head, let's say, they automatically use a 4-iron because that's how far a 4-iron is supposed to go. The manufacturer, or somebody, has determined that to be true but only *in general.* It's absurd to think that everyone hits the ball the same distance with a 4-iron, a 6-iron or whatever. My point is, obviously, that every individual golfer has to find out how far *he* hits the ball with each club in his bag. The yardage marker is only a guide to which he relates his own game!

How do you find out your personal yardage? A driving range with yardage signs is one place. However, those signs are not necessarily correct from the spot where you happen to be hitting balls. Ask the operator of the range where his measurements have been taken from, and hit balls from there if you can.

OK. Let's say there's a 175-yard marker out there. Use your 3-iron and hit 15 or 20 balls at the sign. Then look for your *average length*. Throw out the longest and shortest balls. Where the biggest pile is, is your distance.

Better yet, find your yardage on the golf course itself. Hit shots from a 150-yard marker to determine the club you need to reach that point on the green the course uses for its measurement. Some courses make the measurement from the marker to the front edge of the green, some to the middle and others to the back of the putting surface. Ask the professional where the measurement is made to, although some courses note it on their scorecards.

If a course doesn't have markers or a scorecard with yardage information, step off the distances yourself. You may be taking a step that is not actually a yard—it may be a little longer or shorter—but that makes no difference. As long as your step is consistent every time, it will be *your* measurement related to how far *you* hit your average shot. Get your average distance with every club in the bag when you hit the ball solidly. This might be an enlightening experience in another sense. You may come to realize you don't hit the ball as far as you think. How you deal with that revelation is a mark of how well you want to *play*.

It has been my observation that the better a player is, the more club he takes for shots. The average golfer generally does not take enough club. This may be, in part, because he lets his ego get in his way. But I think it is more often because he is always playing for the perfect shot. I don't believe that's the way to make a good score. How many shots does a 15-handicapper hit squarely? Maybe one out of seven.

So should he play for the one perfect shot or the six misses? Club selection has an important role in the answer to that question.

If you use what you know is enough club for a shot and maybe even a little too much, you will swing smoother and usually hit the ball more solidly. If you happen to hit that one-out-of-seven dead-solid-perfect shot and go over the green, you're generally not too badly off. Most of the trouble around greens is in front and to the sides. And if you don't hit the ball perfectly? Chances are very good you'll still be on the green or pretty close to it. However, when you try to hammer the perfect 6-iron instead of smoothing a 5-iron because you can do a bit of bragging about how strong you are, nine times out of 10 you'll end up in trouble. What's more, the trouble is not simply having put one particular shot in a bunker or out-of-bounds. Pressing for perfection and failing can produce a negative feeling in yourself that can affect a whole string of shots and whole rounds of golf.

It's a cliche, I know, but worth repeating. Know yourself and play within yourself. Don't muscle the ball! Actually, with my swing concept you will hit the ball farther and more consistently anyway, because you're swinging in balance and with an evenly paced tempo.

A realistic approach to the game

Club selection, then, is not simply a matter of knowing the distance and choosing a club to get the ball there. It is also a reflection of the attitude you have toward your game. I think an awful lot of average golfers think too much about hitting the ball and not enough about making a good score. They don't realize how difficult it is to hit a real good shot, and get frustrated when they miss one or don't hit as many good ones as they think they should. As I mentioned earlier, even the best players in the world don't hit every shot well *and don't expect to.* So why should you be afraid to miss one, or be totally dismayed when you do?

Most of us are impressed by statistics and try to learn from them. Well, consider this. As I write this, Calvin Peete is one of the most accurate players in the game from tee to green. His greens-hit-in-regulation average is 72 percent, which is roughly 13 greens a round. That means the most accurate golfer in the world is missing five greens a round. I'm sure Calvin would love to hit all 18 greens every time he plays, but he recognizes the fact that he won't and does all he can to recover and save strokes on the holes where he misses.

Now, an 18-handicapper is not supposed to hit any greens in regulation, but he'll probably hit two or three, and on a good day four or five. The trouble is, when he misses greens he frets about not having hit the ball well and doesn't pay attention to his pitching, chipping and putting, which are the recovery arm of his game. He ends up making a 6 or 7 or an 8 on the hole instead of a 5 or 4.

If an 18-handicapper gets to where he never makes more than a 5 on a hole, the worst score he shoots is a 90. Chances are he'll do better than that. Gradually he becomes a better golfer. Jack Nicklaus has put this idea well in discussing how he designs his golf courses. He said that on every course he builds, if a 10-handicapper plays it like a 10-handicapper should, he will shoot his handicap or better almost every time. If he tries to play it like a 6-handicapper, he will probably shoot only his handicap and maybe even higher. On his courses, Jack gives every golfer a road to where

he can make *his* score on each hole.

In other words, you don't play for the par marked on the scorecard but for *your par* on every hole.

All that makes a lot of sense, so it comes down to what you want out of the game. Many people want to feel aggressive and that they are not backing off from the challenge of golf. They can. I think the game should be played as offensively as possible. But there should be some restraint, too.

What is offensive (aggressive) and what is defensive (restrained) golf? You can say, "OK, there is trouble on the right and I don't want to get into it." That is purely defensive golf. It's better to say, *"I want to play there—where there's no trouble."* Make the last thought going into the shot a positive, aggressive one, and you'll have a much better chance of making an effective swing, and a lower score.

There is another way to make the point. Let's say you have a 7-iron shot to a pin that is tucked behind a big bunker or a pond. If you have a good lie, go for it! If that same situation calls for a 2-iron and the lie is not very good, play safely for a bogey with a chance to make a par after a good chip and putt. I believe in gambling, but only from good situations! If I have a 60-40 chance of making a difficult shot, I'll try it two-thirds of the time.

I don't mean to be dogmatic about this. Sometimes a situation demands that you take a long chance, and you should go ahead. But you must be ready to accept the consequences.

Playing for a pitch and a putt to save a par can be exciting. You have to use your imagination. And it can often turn a match your way without your having done anything spectacular. An opponent can be up on the green, laughing and giggling after playing two nice shots, while you're pitching or chipping to save a par. But every time you get the ball up and down and save a par, he gets more frustrated. He may start three-putting, and you win. It is a definite psychological lift to get the ball up and down from around the greens. I don't understand why golfers don't pay more attention to that.

That doesn't apply only to the average golfer, either. I often use the example of Jack Nicklaus' first round in the 1980 PGA Championship in Rochester, N.Y., and what happened after that. His first round was beautiful. He missed only one fairway and a couple of greens but shot 70. He complained that he was hitting the ball well but not getting enough out of it. The next day he played like a dog, for him, hitting only eight or nine greens. But he had a chip-in and a lot of other saves from around the greens, and shot 69. As a result, his energy level went way up. He had his adrenaline pumping. He went on to win the tournament, and I like to think it was that second round that made the difference.

Admittedly, you can never feel very confident when you're not swinging well. But sometimes when the swing is working and you're hitting one perfect shot after another, you can fall asleep with boredom. I can hear you saying now, "Oh yeah, let me have some of that boredom," and "Who do you think you're kidding?" To be sure, not many golfers get into a position of hitting one fine shot after another, but I still think it is an awful lot of fun scrambling around saving pars, with great shots from bunkers, fine pitches, a smoothly stroked 40-footer that curls into the cup. The unexpected can be a great source of joy and also develop a positive momentum.

Have a plan, draw a picture

A lot of golfers don't think about the *next shot*! But that's at the heart of the game. Look at the good pool or chess player. He is always thinking ahead. That's the way good golf is played, too.

You are always going to be more successful in the long run if you have a plan for every shot, even if it fails occasionally. I think many golfers get upset with poor shots and simply blame bad

swing mechanics. They should realize that bad swing mechanics often are the result of not thinking about where and how they want the ball to go, and why. Somehow, when the purpose of a swing is more than merely getting the ball properly airborne, the shot is always better.

Having a plan involves strategy, which is the intellectual part of the game. Creating a visual image is the artistic side of it. The intellectual part is involved in calculating distance, weather conditions, the contour of the terrain. The artistic side makes a picture with it all, adding instinct to the mix. You can play golf with only one or the other, but the best golf is played when the two are a team.

Positive practice

Golf practice comes in three different packages. There is the warm-up before starting a round, the preshot routine during the round, and the session when you work on various parts of your swing seeking to learn and improve your long-term performance.

The preround warm-up

I'm not going to dwell on the fact that everyone should hit a few balls on the practice range before starting a round of golf. Everyone can appreciate that loosening up the muscles and joints is necessary. However, I will make a point many golfers don't seem to be aware of; that is, the warm-up should be only that, it is not the time when you work on swing mechanics. You should hit balls only to develop a good rhythm and swing pace.

To establish rhythm and pace, hit more shorter irons so that you won't be tempted to press for distance. Hit a few drivers at the end of the warm-up to stretch yourself to the maximum, but after you do, wind down the session with some short pitches and chips. The thing all great players have is the ability to carry the rhythm and pace they develop on the practice tee to the course. Pay attention to your tempo, and you have a better chance of taking it into your round.

Your concern with aiming and hitting for certain distances is not as great, but you should always be aware of what your ball is doing in the air. If you're drawing the ball during your warm-ups, that is probably going to be your shot for the day, so be prepared to play it during the round.

It is also a good idea in the warm-up to mimic your preswing routine—the way you get into address when playing on the course. Don't just beat out some balls. Get behind the ball for each practice shot, pick out a target area, walk into address and take the positions exactly as you do when playing on the course. This also helps you establish your rhythm. The idea is to prepare yourself so that when you get on the course it is not a foreign experience. Make your warm-up a rehearsal, not just practice.

It also helps allay tension when you're in a pressure situation on the course to have a simple routine to go through. When you go through a familiar pattern of activity you are comfortable, and it gives you a sense of self-confidence. Get into the pattern on the practice tee.

People will say they don't see the pros warming up that way on the practice tee. In many cases that's true, which is why I maintain that 70 percent of the warm-up practice the pros do is not as productive as it should be.

After the ball-hitting warm-up, always stroke a few putts on the practice green. Here again, work primarily on a rhythmic, even-paced stroke and the system you use for getting up to a putt. You'll probably putt for a hole, but a mark on the green would do just as well. You can concentrate better on tempo. In any case, make most of your practice putts no longer than 12 feet. As I mentioned earlier, that's the length from which you can reasonably expect to make putts. A 12-footer is long enough to give you a feel for the speed of the greens with a stroke of sufficient length. And if a few go in, you start the round with a positive psychological feeling.

Preshot practice

This involves the rehearsal swings you should take before getting up to play your shots during a round. It is a very simple business and follows my basic precept for every golf swing...make it even-paced. With the rehearsal swing you imitate the *feels* you're after when it's "show time." Try to simulate mechanics as much as you do the tempo and synchronization of the swing.

Practice practice

Work on swing technique is more productive when done in short, concentrated sessions. Long periods of ball hitting are fine to relieve the frustrations and tensions of life in general, and if you stand there just hammering at balls long enough you may eventually find some timing and rhythm that will produce decent shots. But such sessions are invariably worthless in terms of developing a swing you can use on the golf course.

For one thing, on the golf course you are hitting a shot about every five minutes. But on the practice range the tendency is to hit a ball every 30 seconds. That's one reason why I think no practice session should be over an hour long, that you shouldn't hit a great number of balls and that there should be a reasonable pause between each shot. I don't expect you to hit a practice shot every five minutes, but you want to come as close as you can to simulating on-course conditions. Then, too, each practice shot tends to be hit with thought and purpose—you're more likely to concentrate well on each

swing, and the work becomes productive.

With the exception of tour pros who through constant practice build up golf strength and stamina, golfers cannot usually sustain themselves physcially for more than an hour of practice. Every individual has his own level of physical endurance, and some people may be able to practice a little longer than others, but a person should quit when he finds himself not thinking about each shot he hits and/or feels he is no longer able to put out a maximum physical effort. Thoughtless and tired golf swings on the practice range make the session counterproductive. The muscles are left with a poor "memory," and there is no psychological benefit, either, from leaving the range frustrated.

It pretty much follows that if each practice session is going to be relatively short and concentrated, then at each one you can work on only one element of your swing—at most two. Go into each practice session with a single thought. When you're satisfied that you have reached a goal with the work, leave. If you've reached that goal after hitting only 40 balls, still leave. Don't get into another idea. Go chip and putt. Or better yet, go play.

Putting practice—go for the distance

Putting practice should usually be to find the right stroke tempo, so you don't want to be concerned too much with aiming at a hole. You might make a fairly good-sized circle, or box, and go for that. You are hitting the ball for distance and want to develop a consistent, rhythmic stroke.

If you are going to practice putting for game situations, which means putting for a hole, use only one ball and play it out just as though you were going for a score. Try as many different putts as possible—vary the lengths, breaks, slopes—because on the course no two putts are ever quite the same. The greater the variety of game situations you put yourself in, the better you will be when the game is actually on. For each putt go through your preshot routine and otherwise simulate on-course conditions as much as you can.

Don't make practice-putting sessions too long, either. It can be hard on you physically and mentally. You don't need to hit a lot of practice shots if you're paying attention to each one you do hit.

Chipping practice should follow the same pattern I've described for putting.

A complete practice session, including ball hitting and work around the green, should break down about as follows:

Full swing—45 minutes.
Pitching—15 minutes.
Chipping—15 minutes.
Putting—15 minutes.

This is enough for anyone to improve his game. If you can get in one of those hour-and-a-half sessions a week, that would be ideal. Shorter sessions more often, might be even more productive.

On taking lessons

Golf instruction should be a form of preventive medicine. You go for help before you get sick. I would equate it, also, with taking a car in for a regular 5,000-mile checkup instead of waiting for it to break down before handing it over to the mechanic. In fact, I think *it's more important to go to your teaching professional when you're playing well.* You want to find out what you're doing right and how you can improve on that. You can make such improvements when you're swinging your best, because you have control of your swing. Now your game can truly go forward.

On the same tack, Paul Runyan told me a long time ago to *only change clubs when playing well,* not when playing poorly. His reasoning was, if you do better with a new club when you're hitting the ball well, then you've really got something. Changing equipment when you're going badly is only a crutch, and you want to eliminate as many of them as you can.

I also believe in cram-course instruction, getting the whole picture of what to do all at once, rather than piece by piece. I feel it is a faster and better way to learn. Then, when you do work on only one element of your swing, you can put it in a total context. This tends to make it stick better. It makes more sense to you, and you are less prone to revert to old habits.

For the same reason, I believe a series of lessons should be reasonably close to each other in frequency. After a lesson you will do some practicing on your own, but the pro should check you out every couple of days to be sure you are incorporating the changes. That should be a professional's responsibility, as well as yours. I can take someone and put a Band-Aid on him that will make him hit the ball better. But as soon as the Band-Aid loses its stickum, he is right back where he started. To me, a good golf teacher is someone who carries people to greater heights. It is essentially impossible to do that if the student doesn't come back at frequent intervals. That's also why I think supervised practice is good. It helps the student develop and maintain good habits.

Almost all my pupils have a tendency to regress for a period of time because, first of all, they are making changes. They'll say, "That feels awkward." I say, "Certainly it does, it should because it's different." If I let them be, they are very likely to go back to what feels comfortable, and no progress is made. If I stay with them and supervise their work, they stick with the changes. A lot of students will say they always do much better when I'm there—and that's because they are paying attention when I'm present.

Another thing I've noticed is that students will want to know things about swinging the club they've heard or read about but that have no relationship to what they are doing or want to do. They simply confuse the issue. They also tend to *think* they are doing this or that with the backswing, downswing, pivot, etc., but often are not. That's another reason why supervised practice is a good thing.

What is a pupil's responsibility in taking lessons? First of all, he must want to learn, not just get a Band-Aid. The more you know about the game and the swing, the better you'll play. I don't accept the notion that the less you know about something the better off you are. Instinct is important in playing golf, but instinct is best when it's backed up by hard knowledge. Not all "gut reactions" are the right ones.

Finding your teacher

I think a good teacher is someone with whom you can relate, who defines his ideas in a way that makes sense to you. A good teacher will do everything he can to get through to you and find your "language." If you're an engineering type, he will talk more mechanically about the swing. If you're an artistic type, he will talk to you more in terms of images and feels. All fine instructors care about their students and whether they improve or not. If you have a teacher who cares, you will care, too, and make progress.

Once you find a teacher you're happy with, stay with him. There is nothing worse than going to four or five different teachers and hearing four or five different things. But give the teacher a chance, because he's liable to say the same thing a number of ways until he reaches your understanding. That is what we're trying to develop in our Jack Nicklaus Golf Schools—a consistent teaching program so that players from various clubs who are having problems can tell their professionals they are using a certain system. Then they can explain to the pro what they have been trying to do, and the pro can relate to that instead of putting them onto something alien to their system. Ideally, the professional will be aware of the system.

In a word, stay away from instructional gimmicks! It is important to find a teacher who teaches cause and effect, who can make you understand why certain things are happening in your golf swing. If you're slicing and a teacher tells you only to move your right hand into a different position so you can hook, then you're only getting a Band-Aid. It is not good long-term instruction. The assumption must be that you intend to play the game for the rest of your life. That being the case, you want instruction that will last, a system that holds up over a long period of time. I realize how tempting it is to find a quick solution to an immediate problem. But that is not the way to build a consistent, repeating golf swing.

Taking playing lessons

I don't believe anyone should take only ball-hitting lessons. I think playing lessons are at least of equal value. A playing lesson teaches the scoring part of the game, which is generally left out of golf instruction. People have limits in ball-striking ability, but there is almost no limit to scoring ability.

It is not necessarily the fault of the professional that people don't get enough scoring instruction. Most golfers are overly fascinated with simply hitting the ball and seem to think that what they learn on the practice range automatically transfers to the golf course. It doesn't, as most of you know very well. It is very rare to find people who just like to practice

and who are also good players. A certain amount of habit is a good thing in golf.

The ultimate fascination of golf is the many variations on the theme. No two shots are ever exactly alike—the lie is always a bit different, the wind is in a different direction or there's none at all, it's chilly one day, hot another, and on and on. Being able to adapt to the conditions of the moment is what golf is all about...to adapt within the context of a consistent swing system. If golf were simply standing in one place and hitting balls, it wouldn't be nearly as popular as it is.